Judicial Politics since

Making Contemporary Britain Series

General Editor: Anthony Seldon
Consultant Editor: Peter Hennessy

Published

The British Press and Broadcasting since 1945
Colin Seymour-Ure

Third Party Politics since 1945
John Stevenson

British Science and Politics since 1945
Thomas Wilkie

British Public Opinion
Robert M. Worcester

Forthcoming:

British Industry since 1945
Margaret Ackrill

The Conservative Party since 1945
John Barnes

The British Monarchy
Robert Blackburn

The Labour Party since 1945
Brian Brivati and Andrew Thomas

Electoral Change since 1945
Ivor Crewe and Pippa Norris

Religion in Britain
Crace Davie

British Politics since 1945
Peter Dorey

British Social Policy since 1945
Howard Glennerster

Sport in Britain since 1945
Richard Holt and Tony Mason

Parliament since 1945
Philip Norton

The Trade Union Question in British Politics
Robert Taylor

The Civil Service since 1945
Kevin Theakston

Terrorism since 1945
Paul Wilkinson

Judicial Politics since 1920: A Chronicle

John Griffith

BLACKWELL
Oxford UK & Cambridge USA

First published 1993

Blackwell Publishers
108 Cowley Road
Oxford OX4 1JF
UK

238 Main Street,
Cambridge, Massachusetts 02142
USA

British Library Cataloguing in Publication Data
A CIP catalogue record for this book is available from
the British Library.

Library of Congress Cataloging-in-Publication Data
Griffith, J.A.G. (John Aneurin Grey)
    Judicial politics since 1920 : a chronicle / John Griffith.
        p.   cm. — (Making contemporary Britain)
    Includes bibliographical references and index.
    ISBN 0–631–19052–X (acid-free paper). — ISBN 0–631–19053–8 (acid
-free paper)
    1. Judicial process — Great Britain — History.   2. Political
questions and judicial power — Great Britain — History.   I. Title.
II. Series.
KD7285.G75   1993   92– 44280
320.941—dc20   CIP

Typeset in 11 on 13pt Ehrhardt
by Graphicraft Typesetters Ltd., Hong Kong
Printed in Great Britain
by T.J. Press (Padstow) Ltd, Padstow, Cornwall

This book is printed on acid-free paper

Tempora mutantur et nos in illis

To Barbara,
the centre that holds

Contents

Series editor's preface

John Griffith's volume is the first in the series to be concerned with judges and public law, although Terence Morris's *Crime and Criminal Justice since 1945* covers a related field.

The author is well known for his writing on law, Parliament, and, amongst a student audience, for his influential short book *The Politics of the Judiciary* (1977). Griffith believes that judges are affected in their decisions by subjective facts relating to their peculiar backgrounds and circumstances, and, moreover, that their judgments in the field of public law have at times profoundly affected society.

Britain's contemporary history, therefore, cannot be fully understood without considering Britain's senior judges, and their most significant judicial pronouncements. Individual judges matter. Lord Greene, Master of the Rolls in the period immediately before, during and after the Second World War, is one such key figure, who had essentially a limited view of judicial review of government action. An inactive period followed in the 1950s which came to an end in the early 1960s with promotion of two powerful lawyers, Lords Denning and Reid, heralding a new period of judicial activism (although not as pronounced as in the United States at the same period). A new era of greater judicial restraint followed from the mid-1970s to the mid-1980s, with Lords Diplock and Wilberforce to the fore.

Griffith's book should appeal to the student of politics, law and contemporary history, as well as to the general reader. No understanding of Britain since the First World War can be complete without reading this book.

Anthony Seldon

Preface

Judges are people. Like us, their attitudes are determined by their class, their upbringing and education, their professional life, and their personal experiences. Unlike most of us, but like politicians, these attitudes, reflected in their decisions, have important consequences both for individuals and for society.

Judicial decisions operate in two broad types of case: in private law, where the dispute is between individual persons; and in public law, where the dispute concerns the special powers of public bodies, including Ministers of the Crown and local authorities. This book is about these special powers which are usually conferred by Acts of Parliament. Where dispute arises, it is the function of judges to adjudicate and to decide whether a particular power has been exceeded and, if so, what the remedy should be. In interpreting the statutory provisions, judges have developed principles, changing over time as their attitudes have changed.

The purpose of this book is to interest the general reader in this corner of contemporary history. The method is to select certain examples that, apart from their intrinsic importance, are sufficiently cognate to show development in judicial attitudes. The selection of other topics would have shown other developments. The Suez chapter is exceptional and is included as an example of the way legal arguments mesh with policy judgments.

Judges have individual characteristics within common patterns of behaviour. Over the seventy years covered by the examples in the book, some judges have been called conservative and some liberal but these words do not consistently describe the same attitudes. Also, judges can interpret only the legislation that comes before them and over this period of time there have been major shifts of political opinion as different governments have held office and enacted their party programmes. But although judges are inevitably affected by the kinds of legislation they encounter, and though they partake, in different ways, of the political atmosphere of their times, there remain strands of judicial attitudes which persist and are discernible, separate from day-to-day politics. These underlying attitudes are part of the history of our time.

I have been helped in many different ways by many people. Of those outside academia, I thank Louis Blom-Cooper, Frank McCall at the PRO, Alistair Cooke, the late Lord Devlin, Lord Fraser of Kilmorack, the Tyne and Wear Archives Service, and J.A. Vallance White. My special thanks go to Cyril Glasser who read the whole script in its penultimate stage. I greatly benefited from his comments but he is not to be blamed for anything and he certainly does not agree with all my conclusions. My special thanks also go, as ever, to Colleen Etheridge whose professional and technical competence is awesome, and who is such a pleasure to work with.

The principal works of scholarship and reference are Robert Stevens *Law and Politics* (1979), which covers the House of Lords as a judicial body from 1800 to 1976; Louis Blom-Cooper and Gavin Drewry, *Final Appeal* (1972), discussing and analysing the decisions of the Law Lords from 1952 to 1968; editors J.L. Jowell and J.P.W.B. McAuslan, *Lord Denning: the Judge and the Law* (1984), especially the chapter by Claire Palley; Carol Harlow and Richard Rawlings, *Law and Administration* (1984); R.F.V. Heuston, *Lives of the Lord Chancellors 1940–1970* (1987); Alan Paterson, *The Law Lords* (1982). To all these I am indebted, as to the many other cited works on particular subjects. General histories of great value are A.J.P. Taylor, *English History 1914–1945* (1965); Kenneth O. Morgan, *The People's Peace 1945–1989* (1990); Alec Cairncross, *The British Economy since 1945* (1992).

Appendix 1 contains a simplified structure of the courts. Appendix 2 is a note on injunctions.

John Griffith
Marlow

1 Between the wars

The Poplar cases

'Precedents were quoted on either side and at one point the Lord Chief Justice said he could not imagine the reasons for Poplar's action "unless it be popularity", to which Slesser replied: "No, my Lord, I am afraid it is poverty".'[1]

Soldiers from the war returning in 1918 had their minds on Prime Minister Lloyd George's promise of a fit country for heroes to live in, and for a short while standards of living improved. It was confidently expected in Britain that, as controls on prices, raw materials, foreign trade and direction of industry were swiftly relaxed, there would be great demand, both at home and abroad, for goods of all kinds. But prices rose twice as fast during 1919 as they had during the worst years of the war. A.J.P. Taylor wrote that taking 1914 as 100, wholesale prices were over 200 early in 1919 and over 300 early in 1920.[2] Wage rises followed prices. The result was a huge inflationary boom.

The collapse came even more swiftly, during the winter of 1920–1. There followed increased taxation, and considerable reduction of Government expenditure. Between December 1920 and March 1921 unemployment more than doubled and by June 1921 totalled more than 2 million. Wages sharply declined.

The effect in the poorer areas of the industrial cities was disastrous. In the borough of Poplar in the East End of London in 1921 there were 15,000 unemployed out of a total population of 160,000. Since 1919 the Labour party had dominated local politics under the leadership of George Lansbury, at the head of a group of strongly radical men and women.[3]

As a young man Lansbury had been a Liberal, but before the turn of the century he had moved through the Social Democratic Federation to the Independent Labour party and thence to the left wing of the Labour party. In 1892 he became an elected member of the Poplar Board of Poor Law Guardians and in 1903 of Poplar borough council. In 1910 Lansbury was elected as Member of Parliament for the Bow and Bromley Division of Poplar but resigned two years later in protest at the Parliamentary Labour party's failure to support the militant suffragettes. In the ensuing bye-election he stood as an independent socialist and was defeated by the Tory candidate by 751 votes. Votes for women aroused too many antagonisms, for different reasons in different groups in society, in pre-war Britain.

From 1912 to 1922 Lansbury edited the *Daily Herald*. He was continuously a Poplar Guardian from 1904 to 1930, a Poplar councillor from 1903 to 1940, a re-elected Member of parliament for Bow and Bromley from 1922 to 1940 and the Labour leader in the Commons from 1931 to 1935.

The poorer the area the greater were the demands for help from those in need, and the smaller the financial resources. The situation was made worse by the requirements of other authorities which looked to the boroughs to cover their expenditure. These included the London County Council, the Metropolitan Asylums' Board and the Metropolitan Police. They demanded contributions from the boroughs of a uniform precept levied on the value of individual properties in the boroughs. But this value varied hugely. Westminster borough had a rateable value per head of population of £42. Poplar's was £5. The produce of one penny (old style) rate in Westminster was £31,719; in Poplar it was £3,643.

For many years there had been pressure on governments to introduce an equalization scheme under which the richer London boroughs would contribute to the poorer, but nothing substantial had come about. Lansbury and his colleagues decided to take drastic action to increase this pressure. In March 1921 Poplar borough council resolved to refuse to levy the precepts demanded by the LCC and the other two authorities. This was plainly illegal and in July 1921 the Court of Appeal ordered the councillors to reverse their decision. When they refused, thirty-one were arrested for what was technically contempt of court. Their imprisonment greatly embarrassed the Government. Enforcement of the law may gladden the hearts of the righteous but where the conflict is primarily political may greatly impede the finding of a solution. A deal was struck. After six weeks in prison the councillors were released having expressed their profound regret that their action involved them in disobedience to an order of the Court, disclaimed any wish to treat the Court with disrespect, and disavowed any intention whatsoever of contumacy. They also stated that they wished to be present at a conference to be called by the Minister of Health (Sir Alfred Mond) with a view to arriving at a satisfactory solution of the financial difficulties. The councillors did not, however, promise to carry out the order of the Court.

In the event it was agreed that the cost of outdoor relief for the unemployed would be met from a fund to which all London boroughs contributed and this was effected by the London Authorities (Financial Provisions) Act 1921. In the longer term the councillors' campaign helped towards the general adoption of equalization schemes and the provision of differential government grants. In their actions, the Poplar councillors were widely supported within the borough. But these events also revealed the differences of opinion, perhaps of political philosophy, certainly of political strategy and tactics, that existed (and continue to exist) within the Labour party.

Lansbury was a radical socialist. On 2 September 1921, he wrote in the *Daily Herald*:

These judges, paid to administer the law have, on their own confession, not merely stretched but smashed all law in ordering us to prison. . . . It is well that organised labour should understand that in the Courts of law all the scales are weighted against us because all the judges administer class-made laws, laws which are expressly enacted, not to do justice but to preserve the present social order. The Poplar case will be remembered most because of the fact that three High Court judges deliberately set themselves to help the

LCC and the Metropolitan Asylums' Board out of the hopeless
mess in which they had landed themselves by making a new law
of their own.[4]

This kind of language and indeed the kind of confrontational
politics used by the Poplar councillors, many trade unionists and
others, the politics of action sometimes using illegal means such
as the refusal to obey the precept demands, greatly disturbed the
constitutionalists within the Labour party. Chief among these was
Herbert Morrison, secretary since 1915 of the London Labour
party and at this time mayor of Hackney, later to be a Cabinet
Minister under Churchill during the Second World War and
under Attlee from 1945 to 1951. His biographer has written that
Morrison struggled successfully against the superficially seductive
but constitutionally dangerous attractions of Poplarism; that he
preferred orderly and tidy machinery to resolve conflicts of interests
and was so loyal to the Whitley council system of collective bargaining through constitutionally established negotiating machinery
that he persuaded Hackney borough council to reduce its wages
to conform to the agreed scale.[5] The conflict between Lansbury
and Morrison was temperamental and tactical, emotional and
emotive. Against Morrison it could be argued that his arguments
were too similar to those of his political opponents. Morrison and
Lansbury agreed that the poverty in the East End of London was
a disgrace. But they differed about the methods to be used to
effect a remedy. Against Lansbury it was said that his methods
were reckless, that they lent support to other militants with whose
aims he had little in common, that in the end they were counter-
productive because likely to antagonize the middle classes whose
support was necessary for Labour's eventual victory. In the language
of today, Lansbury fought for socialism, Morrison for Labourism.

The protest by the Poplar councillors, resulting in their imprisonment, was a major political happening. But, in the evolu-
tion of the relationship between the courts and the powers of
public authorities, a different policy decision by Poplar borough
council was more significant.

Co-ordination in the payment of wages to local authority employees in London was sought in a joint industrial (or Whitley)

council comprising representatives of employers and employees. In March 1920, six grades were agreed, ranging from £3 10s.6d (£3.52) to £4 14s.6d (£4.72) per week. However, in May 1920, Poplar councillors resolved to pay all their employees a minimum wage of £4 a week and this included some women who had been earning less than £2 9s.9d (£2.50). After prices collapsed at the end of 1920, it was estimated that the cost of living fell during the financial year 1921–2 from 176 per cent to 82 per cent above the pre-war level. Poplar, however, continued to fix its minimum weekly wage at £4 during that and subsequent years. In June 1923 the district auditor surcharged the councillors a total of £5,000 being a broad assessment of the payments made in excess of the levels of pay agreed in the joint industrial council, although the actual difference was greater.

The district auditor was a statutory officer appointed by the Government under the Public Health Act 1875 to audit the accounts of local authorities and having power to disallow any item of expenditure which was 'contrary to law' and to recover the amount from those making or authorizing the payment (this being known as surcharging). The power of Poplar borough council, along with other local authorities under the Metropolis Management Act 1855, was to pay its employees such wages as the council thought fit. On the face of it, that was a very wide power indeed. It seemed to give the council an unlimited discretion. How then could any payment be 'contrary to law'?

In exercising their function of interpreting the meaning of statutory words, the courts look first at the context in which the words appear. This is particularly important where the words seem to confer wide discretionary powers on public authorities. Powers are given for certain purposes and relate to certain activities. They should not be used for other purposes or activities. If, for example, the governors of a school are empowered to dismiss teachers, the grounds for dismissal must relate to duties and responsibilities associated with teaching, though that may give rise to its own problems of interpretation. But the courts' powers of interpretation are much wider than this.

In October and November 1923 the High Court heard an application to quash the £5,000 surcharge imposed by the district auditor. It was argued on behalf of the councillors that, there being no misconduct or negligence on their part, they had acted lawfully in continuing the minimum wage despite the fall in the cost of living. The three members of the High Court (Lord Chief Justice Hewart and Lord Justices Sankey and Salter), accepting the wider view of the scope of the auditor's powers, held that the council was in a fiduciary position towards all the ratepayers and must not be 'unduly generous'. The illegality arose because the payments were 'excessive'.[6] The councillors appealed.

The Court of Appeal in the 1920s sat in only two divisions, one of which was a powerful body consisting of the three Lord Justices who heard this case: Atkin, Bankes and Scrutton. Atkin, who as a young barrister had been Scrutton's pupil, went on, as we shall see, to become an outstanding Law Lord. Scrutton had a reputation as a hard rugged man of robust common sense with a heavily ironic style. When in their judgments these two disagreed, Lord Denning has said that they 'fought for the body of Bankes'. When the two agreed, Bankes is recorded as having dissented from them on only two occasions.[7] This case was one of those two.

Lord Justice Scrutton said that Parliament had given the council, an elected representative body, a very wide discretion. He was not prepared to go so far as to say that the council could exercise this discretion entirely as it chose so long as it acted in good faith. There must be a limit to justifiable payments which depended on their relation to work done and its market value. But:

> The question is not whether I should have sanctioned these wages; I probably should not; nor whether the auditor or the Whitley Council would have sanctioned these wages; it is for the Poplar borough council to fix those wages, which are not to be interfered with unless they are so excessive as to pass the reasonable limits of discretion in a representative body.

Lord Justice Atkin agreed. He accepted that the council must not pay wages 'as a dole or as a bribe, or with any object other than that of fairly remunerating the servant'. They were not to use the servant or his wages as a means of 'subverting existing institutions'. But it had not been made out that the wages paid were so unreasonable as to be beyond the powers of the council.

Lord Justice Bankes dissented and the language of his judgment set the tone for the future. He said that the council must have taken wholly extraneous matters into consideration, and that this invalidated their decision. The standard rate of wages in any given locality for any form of labour was ascertainable.

> In the case of the private individual [employer] dealing with his own money it is not only competent to him, but it is a humane and praiseworthy action, to approach the question of what he shall pay his employees from the point of view of what will enable them to live up to what he considers a reasonable standard of comfort, and to disregard altogether the question of what other people are paying for similar services or the sum for which he could obtain the service. Not so in my opinion when a public authority adopt the same attitude.

He noted that the council had argued that wages should not be related exclusively to the cost of living and that they should act as a model employer. But, to him, these were matters they were not, as a public authority spending ratepayers' money, entitled to take into account.[8]

In April 1925 a further appeal was taken to the Law Lords, who unanimously overruled the majority in the Court of Appeal and reinstated the decision of the High Court.[9] In their judgments, the five Law Lords stressed differing aspects and gave different emphases.

Lord Buckmaster said that the council's decision was to pay £4 as the minimum wage for adult labour without the least regard to what that labour might be.

> It standardised men and women not according to the duties they performed, but according to the fact that they were adults. . . . They have not determined the payment as wages, for they have eliminated the consideration both of the work to be done and of the purchasing power of the sums paid. . . . They did not base their decision upon the ground that the reward for work is the value of the work reasonably and even generously measured, but

... they took an arbitrary principle and fixed an arbitrary sum, which was not a real exercise of the discretion imposed upon them by statute.

Lord Atkinson let fly in one of the most outspoken political judgments ever to come from their Lordships. Referring to the pre-war practice he said

> The vanity of appearing as model employers of labour had not then, apparently, taken possession of the council, nor had the council become such ardent feminists as to bring about, at the expense of the ratepayers whose money they administered, sex equality in the labour market. . . . The council would, in my view, fail in their duty if, in administering funds which did not belong to their members alone, they put aside all these aids to the ascertainment of what was just and reasonable remuneration to give for the services rendered to them, and allowed themselves to be guided in preference by some eccentric principles of socialistic philanthropy or by a feminist ambition to secure the equality of the sexes in the matter of wages in the world of labour. . . . The indulgence of philanthropic enthusiasm at the expense of persons other than the philanthropists is an entirely different thing from the indulgence of it at the expense of the philanthropists themselves.

Lord Sumner said that the district auditor was not confined to asking if the discretion had been honestly exercised. He had 'to restrain expenditure within proper limits. His mission is to inquire if there is any excess over what is reasonable'. He was not obliged 'to leave the ratepayers unprotected from the effects on their pockets of honest stupidity or unpractical idealism'. Lord Sumner said he could find nothing in the statutes which authorized the councillors 'to be guided by their personal opinions on political, economic or social questions in administering the funds which they derive from levying rates'.

Lord Wrenbury took a more semantic approach. He defined 'wages' as the pecuniary return for services rendered. The level of wages could be ascertained by investigating 'the current rate in fact found to be paid in the particular industry'. Anything beyond that was not wages but a gratuity and the council was entitled only to pay wages.

> A person in whom is vested a discretion must exercise his discretion upon reasonable grounds. A discretion does not empower a man to do what he likes merely because he is minded to do so – he must in the exercise of his discretion do not what he likes but what he ought. In other words, he must, by use of his reason, ascertain and follow the course which his reason directs. He must act reasonably.

Lord Carson had 'doubts' but did not dissent. He followed Lord Wrenbury in finding the wages paid to be so excessive as to be gifts and thought the councillors 'were affected by considerations which could not be held to come within the ambit of the discretion entrusted to them'.

Much of the formulation of these opinions was semantic, looking at the dictionary meaning of words and finding, for example, that the payments made to employees were not 'wages'. Yet their Lordships were obviously conscious that they were dealing with an intensely political situation, not of their making. They were asked to adjudicate on the wider interpretation which district auditors had, of recent years, been applying to their statutory powers to disallow expenditure. They took the view that those powers should be broadly defined despite the apparently wide discretion given to elected local authorities to pay such wages as they thought fit. By emphasizing the disassociation (as they saw it) of work done from rate of pay which was implicit in the concept of a minimum wage, especially when this was linked to the council's view of the obligations of a model employer, the Law Lords were able to conclude that the payments were 'contrary to law'.

The radicalism of the Poplar councillors was, no doubt, perceived as a threat. Poplarism had come to mean the resistance of left-wing local authorities to the Governments of the day. These post-war years were full of political upheaval, with widespread strikes and demonstrations. It is not surprising that the House of Lords threw their weight behind the established authority of the centre.

Three of these Law Lords had political backgrounds. Buckmaster had been a Liberal MP for Cambridge from 1906 to 1910 and for Keithley from 1911 to 1915. He was Solicitor-General in 1913 and Lord Chancellor for nineteen months in 1915–16. Atkinson had been Solicitor-General and Attorney-General for Ireland and a Conservative MP for North Londonderry from 1895 to 1905. Carson was MP for Dublin University from 1892 to 1918, Solicitor-General for England 1900–5, Attorney-General 1915–16, First Lord of the Admiralty 1916–18. Sumner was first appointed as a judge in 1909 and promoted rapidly to become a Law Lord in 1913. His many interventions in debates in the House of Lords showed him to be a right-wing Tory. Wrenbury, whose peerage was conferred after he retired as a Lord Justice in the Court of Appeal (so strictly he was not a Lord of Appeal), also spoke in Parliamentary debates in the House but showed personal independence of party.

On 9 April 1925, the Poplar councillors resolved 'under protest and with great reluctance' to consider the whole question of wages with a view to bringing them into conformity with the decision of the House of Lords. And they asked the Minister of Health to set aside the £5,000 and other surcharges. After much further negotiation and additional legislation, a settlement was reached.

Roberts v. *Hopwood* shows the range of weapons in the armoury of the judiciary. Under the guise of seeking 'the intention of Parliament' the courts are able to determine the limits of the statutory powers of public authorities. They may require those powers to be exercised 'reasonably', on their own definition of that word; they may indicate what matters should or should not be taken into account by importing their own notions of what is 'relevant' or what is 'extraneous'; they may bind public authorities to 'fiduciary' duties derived from the common law; they may condemn a decision as 'arbitrary'; they attribute to those authorities motives such as feminism and socialism and then deem them unacceptable; they may invalidate decisions as being 'stupid' or 'idealistic'.

All these criteria are highly subjective and different judges apply them in different ways at different times. The difference of opinion between the majority judges in the Court of Appeal and the Law Lords in *Roberts* v. *Hopwood* emphasizes this subjectivity.

More importantly, judicial attitudes change over time. Some of the cases discussed below would have been decided otherwise at earlier or later times. The political temper of the early 1920s influenced the Law Lords. Lord Justice Atkin did not think the Poplar councillors' actions were intended to be a means of 'subverting existing institutions'. Perhaps the Law Lords were not so sure. Had the events occurred in the 1930s, the view of the majority in the Court of Appeal might have prevailed. Had they occurred in the 1980s, I doubt whether the Court of Appeal would have found for the councillors.

Of the eleven judges who participated in *Roberts* v. *Hopwood*, nine took one view and two took another view. That these two were Atkin and Scrutton was not so surprising. Atkin, by his upbringing and education, was an untypical judge.[10] Scrutton was, of the judges of his time, one of the most aware of the nature of the society he lived in. In a much quoted address delivered to the University of Cambridge Law Society on 18 November 1920 he said:

> The habits you are trained in, the people with whom you mix, lead to your having a certain class of ideas of such a nature that, when you have to deal with other ideas, you do not give as sound and accurate judgments as you would wish. This is one of the great difficulties at present with Labour. Labour says 'Where are your impartial judges? They all move in the same circle as the employers, and they are all educated and nursed in the same ideas as the employers. How can a labour man or a trade unionist get impartial justice?' It is very difficult sometimes to be sure that you have put yourself into a thoroughly impartial position between two disputants, one of your own class and one not of your class.[11]

The general strike

By 1925, there was economic recovery with total industrial production in that year being some 10 per cent higher than in 1913 and more people in work than ever before, as A.J.P. Taylor records.[12] But over one million were unemployed and the remedy

decided on (and persisted in as we shall see) was to lower wages
leading, it was hoped, by reducing prices to an increase in exports.
The coal industry was the largest employer with more than one
million workers and it was being undercut in European markets.
The mine owners demanded lower wages and longer hours. The
General Council of the Trades Union Congress supported the
miners in the hope, perhaps, of forcing the Government to intervene between the National Union of Mineworkers and the
owners. A Royal Commission was appointed in July 1925 and
reported in March 1926. It recommended re-organization of the
industry but also an immediate wage reduction. On 1 May 1926
the miners were locked out by the mine owners. The General
Council called a national strike which began at midnight on 3
May and was widespread. The Government had made preparations
under the guidance of Sir John Anderson, Permanent Under-
Secretary at the Home Office.

On Thursday 6 May, Sir John Simon MP spoke in the House
of Commons. A former Attorney-General and a former Home
Secretary, Sir John was a Liberal MP who still perhaps had hopes
of leading his party in the future. He argued that the general
strike was unlawful as the workmen had 'terminated their en-
gagements' without giving due notice to their employers. The
decision of the General Council of the Trades Union Congress to
call out everybody was not, he said, a lawful act, and every workman
who obeyed it had broken the law. The general strike was 'a
novel and an utterly illegal proceeding'. Thus every railwayman
on strike was 'personally liable to be sued in the County Court
for damages'. Sir John went further and said that every trade
union leader who had advised and promoted the strike was 'liable
in damages to the uttermost farthing of his personal possessions'.
He emphasized in what he called 'a perfectly dogmatic statement'
that no trade unionist who refused to obey the order of his union
to strike would lose any benefits payable under a rule of the
union because the order would be unlawful. 'It cannot be too
widely and plainly known', said Sir John, 'that there is no court
in this country which would ever construe such a rule as meaning
that the man would forfeit his benefits if he is asked to do that
which is wrong and illegal.'[13]

The following Monday (10 May) the Cabinet met at 4.30 p.m. and agreed that the Prime Minister (Mr Baldwin) should arrange for a question and answer in the House of Commons the next day to the following effect:

Q: Does the Government intend to deal with the position of the Trades Unions?

A: The Government are not now contemplating any modifications in existing trade union legislation, but they are considering the desirability of making clear what they believe to be now the law, namely, that a general strike is illegal.

That Monday evening Sir Henry Slesser, who had been Solicitor-General in the Labour Government of 1924, replied in the House (against the wishes of his leader Ramsay MacDonald) to correct what he believed to be 'an erroneous view of the law'. He deplored Simon's introduction of 'highly debatable' questions of law which, he said, should be discussed in the Law Courts and not in Parliament.[14] Sir John responded at 6 p.m. the next afternoon[15] and was able strongly to buttress his arguments with quotations from a judgment delivered that very morning by Mr Justice Astbury in the Chancery Division of the High Court. When the Cabinet met (also at 6 p.m.), their attention was drawn to this judgment. The Prime Minister informed his colleagues that, as a result of a consultation with the Earl of Birkenhead, a Cabinet colleague, 'following the receipt of certain information' he had earlier decided not to implement the Cabinet decision to arrange for a question and answer in the House of Commons.

The case before Astbury arose because although the National Sailors' and Firemen's Union did not support the strike their Tower Hill branch officials had called out their members in support of the TUC. The Union asked for a declaration and an injunction to restrain their officials. In the course of his judgment Mr Justice Astbury said:

The so-called general strike called by the Trades Union Congress Council is illegal, and persons inciting or taking part in it are not protected by the Trade Disputes Act 1906. No trade dispute has been alleged or shown to exist in any of the unions affected, except in the miners' case, and no trade dispute does or can exist between the Trades Union Congress on the one hand and the Government and the nation on the other.

Astbury went on to say that no member of the Union could lose his trade union benefits by refusing to obey unlawful orders. An injunction was issued.[16]

It seems that the case was first heard by Astbury on 6 May, on the evening of which day Sir John Simon made his first speech, declaring the general strike unlawful. Then, the day after Sir Henry Slesser's attack, Astbury delivered his judgment which strongly supported Sir John's position and provided judicial authority for Sir John's second speech that same evening. It is difficult to believe that the judge and the politician were not sharing their thoughts on this matter. It seems likely that they knew one another well. Astbury had been a fellow Liberal MP for four years having been first returned at the same time as Simon during the Liberal victory of 1906; and he was made a judge in 1913 during Simon's five-year period as Solicitor-General and then Attorney-General.

Opinions differ greatly about the importance of Simon's speeches and Astbury's judgment. It is said that Astbury claimed more than once that his contribution had saved the nation.

One view is that the TUC leaders were genuinely concerned at the allegation that they were acting illegally. But the reality may be more complex. Individuals may defy a particular law and be applauded for doing so where either the law or its application is seen as unjust. Opposition political parties may condemn particular laws, as Labour attacked the poll tax in the United Kingdom in the late 1980s. But the Opposition leaders must take great care not to be seen to advocate disobedience. If they do, they enable their opponents to accuse them of disregarding the rule of law itself and so rendering themselves unsuited for government. There is a general consensus that 'the law' should be upheld while particular laws may be attacked. The General Council of the TUC may have been more affected by the way its image might be darkened in the view of the non-striking public if it seemed to be defying 'the law' than worried about the prospects of actions being brought in the courts against its members or against individuals on strike. The charge of illegal or 'unconstitutional' action brought by Ministers against the General Council and the strikers generally was intended more as a political manoeuvre than as a threat of litigation. There were undoubtedly more important reasons why the TUC called off the general strike on 12 May.

Despots and conceptualists

We have seen how judges, when interpreting legislation, sometimes restrict the apparent meaning of words giving powers to public authorities so as to make their exercise conform to certain criteria adopted by the courts. So the power 'to pay such wages as the council think fit' is restricted by asserting that such wages must be 'reasonable' or not based on 'extraneous' considerations. A similar limitation has long been placed on the procedure by which public authorities arrive at certain decisions. They must, it is said, act in accordance with the rules of natural justice. At the beginning of this century, this was applied particularly when government departments were empowered by statute to decide disputes arising between local authorities and private persons. In *Board of Education* v. *Rice* in 1911[17] the Board had power to determine a question regarding the discrimination made by a local education authority against a school in the matter of salaries. The Lord Chancellor said that the Board must, of course, act in good faith and fairly listen to both sides. But the Board need not examine witnesses, as a court did. The Board could obtain information in any way they thought fit, so long as the parties were given an opportunity to correct or contradict statements likely to prejudice their case. The obligation to hear both sides fairly is the principal rule of natural justice. But although the Lord Chancellor insisted on this rule being observed, he implicitly recognized the power of the Board to determine not only what were the facts but also what was the applicable law and to decide accordingly. From such a decision so arrived at there was no right of appeal to the courts unless the legislation expressly so provided.

A few years later in 1915 the Law Lords decided *Local*

Government Board v. *Arlidge*.[18] Here Hampstead borough council
had made a closing order on a house which appeared to be unfit
for human habitation, in accordance with their statutory powers.
A local inquiry was held, conducted by an inspector from the
department, after which the Minister confirmed the order. The
owner of the house sought to have this decision invalidated on
the grounds that he was not told which of the officials in the
department had actually decided the appeal; that he had not had
an opportunity of being heard orally by that official; and that he
was not allowed to see the report of the inspector. The Law
Lords rejected these claims on the ground that a government
department entrusted by an Act of Parliament with the exercise
of such functions need not follow the procedures adopted by the
courts so long as the department acted fairly and judicially.

Such decisions handed down by the highest court were evidence of the trustworthiness with which the executive organs of
government were regarded by judges. But the feeling was not
universal even among those on the bench. In 1929 Lord Hewart,
who was then Lord Chief Justice of England, wrote and published a book entitled *The New Despotism* which drew attention to
the dangers, as seen by the author, of the increase in governmental power and particularly that of the members of the civil service.
Lord Hewart feared that the two bulwarks of the English constitution – the sovereignty of Parliament and the Rule of Law –
were being progressively weakened. The previous year a quite
different book – scholarly and analytical – had addressed the same
questions but W.A. Robson's *Justice and Administrative Law* did not
attract the same publicity.

In 1929 the Lord Chancellor, Lord Sankey, appointed the
Committee on Ministers' Powers which reported in 1932.[19] This
was a powerful Committee of seventeen members at first chaired
by Lord Donoughmore and then by Sir Leslie Scott. It was heavily
stocked by the Great and the Good with senior barristers and
senior civil servants, the latter including the Permanent Secretary
to the Lord Chancellor's department (Sir Claud Schuster), the
Permanent Under-Secretary at the Home Office (Sir John
Anderson, whom we have already met[20] and will meet again, ten
years on) and the Permanent Secretary to the Treasury (Sir Warren

Fisher). There were, however, two unusual members: Professor Harold Laski of the London School of Economics and Political Science whose views would have been considered dangerously radical by most of his colleagues on the Committee; and Ellen Wilkinson, the left-wing Labour MP.

The terms of reference of the Committee reflected Lord Hewart's concerns. They were to consider the powers exercised by or under the direction of Ministers of the Crown by way of (a) delegated legislation and (b) judicial or quasi-judicial decision; and to report what safeguards were desirable or necessary to secure the constitutional principles of 'the sovereignty of parliament and the supremacy of the Law'. The variety of meanings attached to these last two phrases was bound both to beg a number of questions and to pre-empt many of the conclusions.

The Committee was therefore required to consider situations in which Ministers (or other public bodies) made decisions which were judicial or quasi-judicial. So it was forced to define these terms and to distinguish their meaning from a third category called administrative. The implication was that special restrictive rules ought to be applied to judicial or quasi-judicial decisions from which administrative decisions would be free. The Committee found that a 'true judicial decision' presupposed an existing dispute, the presentation of their case by the parties, a finding of the facts and of the applicable law, and a decision by the adjudicating body based on those findings. A quasi-judicial decision differed in that the last stage was administrative action 'determined by the Minister's free choice'. In contrast to both of these, an administrative decision required no such finding by the Minister and 'the grounds upon which he acts, and the means which he takes to inform himself before acting, are left entirely to his discretion'. The Committee said that the rules of natural justice applied to judicial and quasi-judicial decisions. So there must be no 'bias' or interest in the decision-maker who must also give a fair hearing to the two sides to the dispute. But this did not apply to the administrative decision.

It did not take long for the artificiality of these distinctions to be exposed but their persistence bedevilled the emergence of realistic principles for some thirty years. Great emphasis was placed on the need for there to be a 'dispute' – a *lis inter partes* – for a decision to be classified as quasi-judicial. Housing legislation became the testing ground.

Housing and the courts

During the twenty years (1919–39) between the world wars, the living conditions of the poor were determined by two main factors: housing shortage, insanitary conditions and slums; and unemployment.[21]

In June 1919 Christopher Addison became Minister of Health in Lloyd George's coalition cabinet. The Housing and Town Planning Act of that year encouraged local authorities to build houses and to let them at low rents, the Government meeting all costs in excess of a penny rate, once Ministry approval had been obtained. This almost open-ended policy proved expensive. It also conflicted, over a longer term, with the Conservative view that the housing shortage was temporary and that private enterprise would soon be able to supply adequate housing at reasonable rents. Addison was transferred in March 1921 and Sir Alfred Mond became Minister of Health in time to be confronted by the Poplar councillors.[22] In July 1921 the subsidies were greatly reduced and a limit of 170,000 houses, imposed on the programme, was expected to be reached by July 1922.

A new policy had to wait until the implementation of the Housing Act 1923 by which time the Minister of Health was Neville Chamberlain in Bonar Law's Cabinet. The subsidy was now set at a maximum of £6 per annum for twenty years, preference being given to private enterprise building, the houses to be built by 1 October 1925, again in the belief that the housing crisis could be sharply overcome. In January 1924 Ramsay MacDonald formed the first Labour Government. Charles Wheatley was Minister of Health and, in the Housing (Financial Provisions) Act of that year, he reversed Chamberlain's policy, increasing subsidies by 50 per cent payable for forty years, the houses predominantly to be built by local authorities for rent and the programme to continue for fifteen years. Although the subsidies were reduced by the Conservative Government in the mid 1920s, Wheatley's general policy, consolidated in the Housing Act 1925, persisted until the financial crisis of 1931–2.

The serious unemployment of the 1920s led to a demand for public works, including housing, to be promoted in the worst areas. As early as 1909 the Minority report of the Royal Commission on the Poor Law had proposed that the Government should earmark a definite proportion of its normal capital expenditure to finance a programme of public works.[23] In December 1920 an Unemployment Grants Committee was appointed to administer a scheme of financial aid to local authorities but it was not successful and was effectively closed down in July 1926. However, public works were accepted by the Conservative Government by 1928 as one means of reducing unemployment and the Public Works Facilities Act 1930 sought to improve procedures, especially for the compulsory purchase of land for building, this having long been a necessary, though controversial, power of public authorities. The UGC was briefly revived but, overall, public works seem to have made little impact on unemployment before the financial collapse of 1931.

Behind these developments lay deep political differences on the appropriate or effective limits which should be placed on government activity. In 1924, the Liberal leader Lloyd George called for a large-scale programme of public works and the economist J.M. Keynes was, more broadly, calling for more investment at home as a solution to national problems. By the end of the 1920s, the policy of the Liberal party was for more spending on roads, bridges, house building and much else while the Conservatives saw revival as coming mainly from the expansion of overseas trade. The Labour party argued for long-term plans of national development and the rejuvenation of industry in a socialist society; they put little emphasis, except for the short term, on schemes for public works. The strongest advocate for a managed economy was Oswald Mosley whose views were rejected by the Labour party in 1930.

The conventional wisdom of the time – and not only of that time – was that exports must be increased, and that costs (which primarily meant wages) must be reduced as the only way to reduce prices and improve competitiveness in world markets. Public works, at best, were seen by the Treasury as an exercise in damage limitation, of some value in depressed areas. Expenditure on public works by central and local authorities actually fell by 35 per cent in the four years after 1929.

Garside quotes the National Government's Health Minister in September 1932: 'Work could not be provided without capital and capital must be conserved for use in the restoration of industry', a minimalist view supported by economists like Gregory, von Hayek, Plant and Robbins. By this time Keynes, on the other side, was pouring scorn on those who believed 'that we can save up our economies against a later day' when finance permitted. Savings, he said, are 'the one thing which will not keep. If they are not used in capital development pari passu they disappear forever in doles, deficits and business losses.'[24] But this was a minority view and greater expenditure on house-building programmes was not seen as a means of stimulating the economy.

Nevertheless in the early 1930s, the annual reports of the Ministry of Health (at that time responsible for housing policy) recognized that to build houses primarily to overcome the overall shortage of accommodation was not enough. A start had to be made to clear slum areas and to reduce gross over-crowding. It had been hoped that these two problems would be solved as a result of the increase in house building for general needs, especially by the private sector. We still hear the view today that by increasing provision for the well-to-do, the poor will benefit indirectly. Evidence for this is less easy to find.

The twelfth Annual Report of the Ministry of Health (for 1930–1) referred to 'a considerable amount of evidence available, in the reports of Medical Officers of Health and elsewhere, that there has been discouragingly little improvement in the worst cases of overcrowding and unhealthy conditions'. The conclusion, said the Report, was inescapable 'that the general filtering up process had been retarded by certain factors, for which perhaps insufficient allowance had been made, and that the indirect method of improving the housing of the poorest classes had to this extent fallen short of expectation'.[25]

Some attempt at slum clearance had been made in the 1920s.

Legislation, consolidated in the Housing Act 1925, made provision for improvement and reconstruction schemes which could, if the Minister confirmed, deal with unhealthy areas. But two decisions of the courts had, by the late 1920s, brought to a standstill even this small programme.

The first of these cases arose from an improvement scheme in the city of Derby.[26] Under the Act of 1925, the local authority, after reports from their Medical Officer of Health, resolved that a very small area of 1¼ acres was 'unhealthy' within the meaning of the Act. The scheme, published and submitted to the Minister, empowered the local authority, if the scheme were approved by the Minister after a public local inquiry, to acquire the land and sell, lease or otherwise dispose of the cleared area or use it for any purpose approved by the Minister. If the Minister so required, the local authority was to provide up to seventy two dwellings for the working classes within or outside the area. The owners applied to the courts for an order prohibiting the Minister from considering the scheme on the ground that the scheme should have provided particulars of the proposed development of the area and not conferred on the local authority an unrestricted power to sell or lease the land. The Court of Appeal in March 1929 upheld the decision of the Divisional Court of the King's Bench Division and granted the owners' application. Lord Hewart CJ put it this way:

> The real substance of the complaint is that under the name, and the agreeable name, of an improvement scheme, this particular council is minded to acquire a slice of very valuable land in the heart of the city of Derby, not for any purpose of rearrangement or reconstruction but for the purpose, if and when the local authority thinks fit, of resale and, of course, of resale at the highest obtainable price.

The second case was an improvement scheme in Liverpool.[27] The landowners claimed that at the statutory local inquiry into the scheme no proper plans showing the proposal layout were produced nor were such plans submitted to the Minister; also that the scheme contained a clause giving the local authority power

to appropriate the land, where not used for working-class housing, to such public purposes as the local authority might direct,
or to sell, lease or otherwise dispose of it as they thought fit. The
Minister modified the scheme to make it accord with the decision
in *ex parte Davis*. But again the Court of Appeal in March 1930
held that the scheme was invalid.

The effect of these two decisions was that local authorities
were deterred from proceeding with improvement schemes for
fear of liability to excessive compensation. As interpreted by the
courts the procedure had become too complicated and gave too
many opportunities for obstruction and delay. In March 1931,
the Law Lords overruled the Court of Appeal in *Yaffe* but up to
two years' delay had ensued.[28]

As often happens, the courts in these decisions came late in the
day to interpretations which conflicted with long-standing administrative practices as followed and understood. For more than
fifty years, comparable schemes giving similar powers to dispose
of land acquired by public authorities had been in force under
procedures approved by Parliament.[29]

A further impediment to progress under the Act of 1925 were
judicial decisions that the powers to purchase slum property given
under an improvement or reconstruction scheme lapsed if not
fully exercised within three years. It had previously been assumed
that the statutory limitations were satisfied if the owners of such
property had received within the prescribed period a 'notice to
treat'.

The second Labour Government was formed in June 1929.
The new Minister of Health was Arthur Greenwood, later to be
for a time a member of Winston Churchill's War Cabinet and a
member of Attlee's Labour Cabinet in 1945. The Housing Act
1930 revised the procedure for slum clearance schemes and sought
to stimulate new programmes. The difficulties created by the judicial decisions were largely removed by this legislation. The Act
introduced subsidies payable in accordance with the numbers of
people displaced and re-housed from slum properties. There were
also variations for agricultural and urban areas and where the cost
of acquiring and clearing sites was high. Local authorities were
expected to make contributions from their rate fund and to fix

appropriate rents. Plans were to be made for housing over five-year periods and submitted to the Minister.

The Housing Act of 1930 provided that where a local authority were satisfied as respects any area in their district (i) that the dwelling houses in that area were, by reason of disrepair or sanitary defects, unfit for human habitation; or were by reason of their bad arrangement, or the narrowness or bad arrangement of the streets, dangerous or injurious to the health of the inhabitants of the area; and that any other buildings were similarly dangerous or injurious to the health of the inhabitants; and (ii) that the most satisfactory method of dealing with the conditions in the area was the demolition of all the buildings, then the local authority should pass a resolution declaring the area to be a clearance area to be cleared of all buildings. But before passing such a resolution the local authority should satisfy themselves that accommodation could be provided for those displaced and that the resources of the authority were sufficient to carry the resolution into effect.

The local authority were then required to clear the area either by ordering the demolition of the buildings or by purchasing the land and themselves demolishing the buildings.

After the resolution had been passed, the local authority were to make a Clearance Order which defined the area and were to send this Order to the Minister of Health for his confirmation or otherwise. He could amend the Order but not so as to extend the area defined. Clearance Orders had to be publicized and objections (usually by owners of affected buildings) could be made to the Minister. Before the Minister decided whether or not to confirm the Clearance Order, he was required to appoint one of his inspectors to hold a public local inquiry at which the objectors and representatives of the local authority could be heard. The inspector, having also examined the site, then made a confidential report to the Minister with recommendations. And the Minister came to his decision. Finally, any person (typically an objector) could question the validity of an order on the ground that it was not within the powers of the Act or that a requirement (usually procedural) of the Act had not been complied with, by applying to the High Court within six weeks of the Minister's confirmation of the order. The High Court could quash the order if satisfied that it was not within the powers of the Act or that the interests of the applicant had been substantially prejudiced by any requirement of the Act not having been complied with.

Mr Justice Swift was the judge nominated to hear cases under this novel procedure. The first concerned a slum Clearance Order in South Shields.[30] The Order as originally drafted by the local authority purported to require the buildings to be vacated in a period less than the statutory twenty-eight days. The Minister confirmed the Order but modified it to conform with the statutory period. Also, the Order did not, as required by regulations, include a 'starred' note setting out the substance of part of the Act of 1930.

The judge showed his general attitude to expropriation by saying that the owner's case 'should be entertained sympathetically' and that such a statute 'should be construed strictly against the local authority and favourably towards the interest of the applicant'. Nevertheless Swift J decided that neither of the objections invalidated the Order: the first defect had been remedied, and the interests of the applicant had not been substantially affected by the second.

The Errington decision

Of the municipal boroughs in England and Wales (this excluded London and the eighty-three largest cities) set down in the statistics recorded in the twelfth Annual Report of the Ministry of Health (for 1930–1) already referred to, the town of Jarrow promised the most.[31] Its estimated number of houses to be demolished and replaced under the Act of 1930 was 868, involving 4,263 persons. These figures were the largest amongst the 100 or so municipal boroughs listed, the nearest being Walthamstow at 751 and 3,734 respectively.

The fourteenth Annual Report (for 1932–3)[32] concluded that the rate of progress in these early years under the Act of 1930 was too slow, adding as a new reason that in many cases where houses had been included in Clearance Orders owners had offered at the local inquiry to make the houses reasonably fit for human habitation.

Where the houses, although not capable of repair at reasonable expense, had not gone beyond the stage at which effective reconditioning could be carried out, the Minister had sometimes excluded them, leaving it to the local authority to institute proceedings if the owners' undertakings were not properly carried out. Such Ministerial action caused delay.

The social conditions for working-class people in Jarrow in the 1920s and 1930s were amongst the very worst in Britain. A report published in 1933 showed that the percentage of deaths in Jarrow due to tuberculosis was 13.2 compared with 7.5 in England and Wales. The tuberculosis death rate in Jarrow over the five years 1926–30 was greater than in 1896–1900, although the rate for the whole country had fallen by 50 per cent during these two periods. The average proportion of deaths of Jarrow children from all forms of tuberculosis was 24.4 per cent, the corresponding figure for children in urban districts of England and Wales being 10.5. Of families with tuberculosis, 48.9 per cent in Jarrow were undernourished.[33] In 1932–3, Jarrow's total population was 35,000 and its Medical Officer of Health estimated that its unemployment rate was over 80 per cent, with 6,000 on the dole, and 23,000 on poor law relief.[34]

On 23 February 1933, Jarrow borough council made the North Ward No. 1 Clearance Order and submitted it to the Minister of Health for confirmation. The area of 1.73 acres covered by the Order had been scheduled by Jarrow council as unhealthy since 1922, and in April 1933 had 398 residents, a density of 230 persons per acre in ninety-six separate tenements (having a total of 184 rooms), none of them with water laid on. There were congestion, overcrowding and other sanitary defects of which the most serious and widespread appeared to be rising damp, according to the evidence given by the Medical Officer of Health for the borough. During the post-war period, Jarrow had passed through a period of industrial depression without parallel in the town's history, according to its submission in December 1935 to the Royal Commission on Local Government in Tyneside.[35]

On 13 April the council published the notice required by the Act and served it on the owners of the properties comprised within the Order, including the appellants who on 26 April gave notice of their objection to the Order. The grounds of objection included (1) that the dwelling-houses in the area were in good repair and sanitary condition and fit for human habitation (2) that the expense to the council if the Order were confirmed would be more than the town could bear at that time (3) that the council could not provide or secure the provision of accommodation for persons of the working classes who would be displaced within the time specified nor did such accommodation already exist (4) that in any event the demolition of all the buildings in the area was not the most satisfactory way of dealing with conditions in the area.

The Minister appointed Mr Collin, one of his inspectors, to hold a public local inquiry on 31 May and 1 June 1933. At some date thereafter Mr Collin reported to the Minister with his recommendations which were not published.

During the inquiry, the owners of the properties in the area gave undertakings that they would effect necessary repairs. This was viewed, by the council, in the light of the past years, as a death-bed repentance (denied by the owners) but it was no secret that the council had decided to proceed by Clearance Order because they were convinced that this was the best, probably the only, way to ensure that the defects were removed. The owners argued that several of the houses in the clearance area were well capable of being made fit for human habitation and that some were not individually unfit. This was no doubt so but the council insisted that, as the Act said, the most satisfactory method of dealing with the conditions was the demolition of all buildings in the area.

On 6 September, representatives of the council and of the owners met in Jarrow and Mr Collin suggested that the owners should submit particulars of what they were prepared to do. Some agreement appeared to be arrived at, but the full council insisted that the proper way to proceed was by confirmation of the Order and they submitted additional evidence to the Minister. On 13 October, the Medical Officer of Jarrow wrote to the council saying: 'With regard to the area generally, I feel that in view of the low standard of workmanship ... and low quality of the materials used in the construction of these houses it is unlikely that any repair will render the houses fit for a reasonable length of time'. The council sent this letter to the Minister.

On 17 November, the town clerk and Medical Officer of Jarrow met Mr Kerwood from the Ministry and Mr Collin in London. The Ministry officials expressed the opinion that whilst the houses were not then fit for habitation, they could be made so for another fifteen or twenty years by doing very substantial repairs amounting in some cases to reconstruction, and that the owners should be asked to agree to a schedule of works for this purpose. This may have been in part because the Ministry officials were impressed by the weakness of the financial position of Jarrow and doubted whether the resources of the local authority were sufficient for carrying out the Clearance Order. But the council again disagreed and on 3 January 1934 asked the Minister to receive a deputation to reiterate their submission that the demolition of all houses was the only effective method of dealing with the area. On 10 January Mr Kerwood replied: 'I think it will be better to write to you semi-officially. . . . In view of the quasi-judicial function which the Minister has to exercise there would be considerable difficulty in the way of receiving a formal deputation representing one side only', and asked what had been the result of the negotiations with the owners on reconditioning. On 11 January the town clerk told Mr Kerwood that the council would not permit the town's officials to negotiate with the owners.

On 23 January, the Principal Assistant Secretary in charge of housing in the Ministry, with Mr Kerwood and Mr Collin, visited Jarrow and inspected the area in company with the town officials, no representatives of the owners being present. On 24 February the town clerk wrote to Mr Kerwood saying that the council had resolved to adhere to the Order and requested its confirmation. The letter continued that the council had been advised by the borough engineer that it was not practicable to deal with the houses individually by closing order and that he had advised that the foundation and structure of the houses, generally speaking, precluded the possibility of their reconstruction. The engineer had not been called as a witness at the inquiry and those who represented the owners had not had the opportunity to cross-examine him. On 27 March, the Clearance Order was confirmed by the Minister of Health.

On 27 May the owners gave notice of their intention to move the High Court, under section 11 of the Housing Act 1930, for an order that the confirmed Clearance Order should be quashed on the ground, primarily, that their interests had been substantially prejudiced in that, between the holding of the public inquiry and the confirmation, the Minister and the council discussed the condition of the houses, made an inspection, and corresponded, without giving notice to the owners or giving them any opportunity to attend the meetings or see the correspondence.

As we have noted, such cases were at this time first considered in the King's Bench Division by Mr Justice Swift. His view was that the Minister was not acting as a judge deciding an issue between two parties but was acting as an administrative officer having to perform a statutory duty imposed upon him by the legislature for the benefit of the community, and that so long as he complied with all the requirements which the legislature had laid down to govern his conduct when there were objections – by holding a public inquiry and by considering the objections and the report of the person who held the inquiry – he might inform his mind in any way he liked and arrive at his decision in any way which seemed good to him. So he rejected the application by the property owners who appealed to the Court of Appeal.[36]

Before the Court of Appeal, on 11 and 12 October 1934, it was argued on behalf of the Minister of Health that he was entitled to find out the facts for himself and was not confined to the facts put before his inspector at the inquiry; that the relations between the Minister and the local authority were those between a superior and a subordinate administrative body; that the local authority did not act as a slum clearance authority subject to an appeal to the Minister but that both acted together as the slum clearance authority and worked in unison.

Lord Justice Maugham began by saying that the main question of law concerned 'the position which the Minister occupies' under the legislation. Were his acts 'merely acts of administration' or was he 'exercising a quasi-judicial function'? He explained what he meant by 'quasi-judicial' by reference to words used by Lord Loreburn LC in *Board of Education* v. *Rice*.[37] The Minister must act in good faith and fairly listen to both sides, for that was a duty lying upon every one who decided anything. He could obtain information in any way he thought best, always giving a fair opportunity to those who were parties in the controversy for correcting or contradicting any relevant statement prejudicial to their view. In determining whether the position of the Minister in *Errington* was quasi-judicial, Maugham LJ said it was necessary to appreciate that under a clearance area scheme to which objections were made there was a true contest between the owners of the property and the local authority which the Minister had to determine. It also had to be borne in mind, he said, that the rights of the owners were 'very seriously affected' by an Order that their houses (where unfit for human habitation) should be demolished without compensation. He rejected the view that after an inquiry had been held and after a report had been made the Minister could hold 'a private inquiry of his own to which one party only is admitted' into matters which were the subject of an objection definitely put and urged before the inspector at the public inquiry: that of demolition or reconditioning. The judgments of Greer LJ and Roche LJ were on similar lines. So the Clearance Order was quashed.

On 20 and 21 December 1934, two more cases came before Mr Justice Swift. In *Frost* v. *Minister of Health*,[38] the City of Birkenhead had declared a clearance area under the Housing Act 1930, but before going further the City had consulted the Ministry of Health and on their advice excluded certain houses from the Clearance Order. A local inquiry followed at which the owners of certain other properties objected. But the Minister confirmed the Order. The owners applied to the High Court on the ground that the prior consultation invalidated the proceedings. Referring to the Court of Appeal decision in *Errington* Swift J said 'I have not the slightest desire to question that decision which I follow loyally, but I am bound to say that I do not understand it. It seems to me that the whole scheme of the Act is against such a view. . . . It seems clear to me that throughout the Act [the Minister] is acting administratively and not judicially.' He held that up to the time of the owners' objections, the Minister was acting in an administrative not a judicial capacity and so was entitled to advise the local authority. The other case which Swift J heard on the same two days in December 1934 was *Offer* v. *Minister of Health*.[39] We have seen that local authorities had been required to submit five-year slum clearance programmes under the Act of 1930. Kingston-on-Thames asked the Ministry for advice and our friend Mr Collin of *Errington* fame visited the borough, inspected the houses in the proposed clearance area and told the local officials that the houses appeared prima facie to be the class of property other local authorities were including in clearance orders. A local inquiry followed in which Mr Collin took no part, though the fact of his advice was disclosed. Swift J held that there could be no objection to the giving of advice for the same reason he had applied in *Frost*. The Minister, he said, 'was doing his bounden duty under the Act in advising local authorities as to the scope and operation of the Act, and the steps which they could or might take under it'. The Court of Appeal (Greer, Slesser and Roche L JJ) upheld him. Roche referred to Swift's comment of not understanding the Court of Appeal's decision in *Errington* and considered his 'humility' in following that decision as 'undue and perhaps ironical' especially as 'the learned judge shows plainly that he quite well understood the difference between the two cases and expresses the difference so admirably that I desire to approve and adopt his language'.

Retrospect

The Poplar cases arose because a group of socialist councillors decided to take direct action by refusing to levy and collect certain taxes and by taking literally their power to pay such wages as they thought fit. This inevitably involved the courts who were drawn into the conflict and required to adjudicate. In *Roberts* v. *Hopwood* they were obliged to interpret the statute and so to decide what was the scope of the councillors' authority, on what criteria it could be defined, how far motives were relevant, and to what extent the courts were entitled to impose their own standards on the elected body. While these questions were not new, they had not formerly been raised so blatantly in a political context. The eight judgments in the Court of Appeal and the House of Lords showed that there were no simple answers, that some judges were reluctant to interfere with the decisions taken locally by the body invested by statute with the power of decision (as Lord Greene MR was to emphasize in *Wednesbury*[40]), that other judges showed some enthusiasm in making clear their political preferences and in condemning those of others. So judicial attitudes differed. Thirty years later, the Court of Appeal[41] had no time for the doubts and hesitations expressed by Atkin and Scrutton; nor sixty years later, had the Law Lords.[42]

Judicial intervention in the general strike was more clearcut. Mr Justice Astbury, going far beyond what was necessary for his decision, stood firmly alongside the Government in his opposition to the trade unionists and was willing to condemn their actions as illegal. But this was the opinion of one only of His Majesty's judges, although it reinforced the unions' long-standing view that the courts were amongst their enemies.

All this was highly subjective, seeming to depend largely on the views taken by individual judges of the politics of the situation, of where the public interest lay. This is inevitable but attempts were made, as they still are, to regulate this personal discretionary element by laying down guiding principles. So distinctions were sought between 'policy' and 'law', the former to be determined by public authorities, the latter by the courts.

The conceptualist phase in the development of judicial attitudes to the powers of public authorities looks in retrospect like an uneasy compromise between an interventionist and a hands-off approach. Where the situation created by the statutory provisions was seen as 'judicial' or 'quasi-judicial', then the courts would apply strict rules of procedure; when it was seen as 'administrative', then so long as public authorities followed the steps specifically required by those provisions, the courts would not look further. Judges seemed to be fixated on the test of whether there was the triangular situation familiar to them: that is, a dispute between A and B to be resolved by C. This they recognized as a *lis inter partes*, something they were continuously involved in, and so requiring the application of principles followed by the ordinary courts. First among the requirements was the need for a fair hearing for both sides, which again was translated from the legal Latin *audi alteram partem*.

The difficulty was that the dispute arose in the course of a much wider administrative process. In housing cases, where most of the litigation arose, the story began with a declaration of central Government policy supported by Government finance. A housing shortage was to be tackled and slums were to be cleared. Ministers then encouraged local housing authorities to plan ahead. Within the central department, civil servants were given special responsibilities to promote schemes and inspectors were appointed to hold the local inquiries adopted by the Government and incorporated in legislation as a means of settling conflicts between the claims of land and property owners and the local authorities. After considering the inspector's report in each case, someone in the department would decide, in the name of the Minister and in accordance with his policy.

So the Minister and his department were the originators of the policy and the ultimate decision-makers. The department advised local authorities on their schemes, listened to the objections made by the owners, and came to a conclusion. To Mr Justice Swift in *Errington* it was clear that the Minister in his Department was 'not acting as a judge' but was administering its policy, subject to certain procedures imposed by the statute at one point in the whole process. The Minister had followed the required procedures and was not to be restricted in the ways in which he otherwise informed his mind before coming to his decision. Roche's failure to understand Swift's bewilderment at the decision of the Court of Appeal in *Errington* indicates the gap between the two approaches.

The artificiality of the courts' approach is shown by the distinction drawn in *Frost* and *Offer*. There it was held that no challenge could succeed so long as the public authorities, central and local, held their joint consultations before the owners made their statutory objections. So the Court of Appeal drew a line across a single administrative process. Before the *lis inter partes* arose the judges would not interfere; after it was joined they would insist on their own supplementary rules being observed.

If it was a conscious compromise, it satisfied no one and, in particular, it avoided the difficult question whether, in either or both cases, the courts had a role to play in insisting on the fairness of the whole process.

Beyond all this, the courts were evidently troubled by the interference with the rights of private property owners involved in Clearance Orders. The common law was developed in the protection of such rights and in the litigation that surrounded rival claimants to property. If the state was to be empowered to interfere with those rights, especially when no compensation was payable for the destruction of houses declared not to be fit for human habitation, then the exercise of those powers must be carefully scrutinized and any suggestion of procedural impropriety or any infringement of the rules which the courts had invented to protect the landowner should result in the quashing of statutory orders. The social conditions of those living in towns like Jarrow took second place.

During this period between the wars, the courts were forced to consider their role as arbiters between public authorities exercising statutory powers and affected individuals. In *Roberts* v. *Hopwood*, *Errington* and the other housing cases the courts were asked to declare invalid the exercise by locally elected bodies of wide discretionary powers conferred by Parliament. If what those bodies did was within the letter of the law, and there was no suggestion of corruption or fraud, how far could the courts go in applying their own limiting criteria? Could these criteria include judgment on the merits of the actions, on whether they were socially or politically desirable, or 'reasonable', or 'fair'? Was Mr Justice Astbury acting properly in his judicial intervention during the general strike or was this a question, raised again in the Suez affair,[43] of legal arguments being used to advance political causes? The conceptualist approach proved unhelpful because it created too many anomalies and was artificial. What, if anything, could be put in its place?

Before these questions could be answered the war of 1939–45 posed a new set of political and legal problems.

Notes

1   Noreen Branson, *Poplarism 1919–1925* (1979), p. 39; and see
    B. Keith-Lucas 'Poplarism' in *Public Law*, (1962), p. 52.
2   A.J.P. Taylor, *English History 1914–1945* (1965), p. 140.
3   See J. Schneer, *George Lansbury* (1990); Bob Holman, *Good Old George* (1990).
4   Quoted Noreen Branson, *Poplarism 1919–1925* (1979), pp. 50–1.
5   G.W. Jones, 'Herbert Morrison and Poplarism', in *Public Law* (1973),
    p. 11; and see B. Donoughue and G.W. Jones, *Herbert Morrison* (1973), pp. 47, 79.
6   *R. v. Roberts* [1924] 1 KB 514.
7   Geoffrey Lewis, *Lord Atkin* (1983), p. 93.
8   *R. v. Roberts* [1924] 2 KB 695 (May–June 1924).
9   *Roberts* v. *Hopwood* [1925] AC 578.
10 See below, p. 47.
11 1 *Cambridge Law Journal* (1921), p. 8.
12 A.J.P. Taylor, *English History 1914–1945* (1965), p. 238.
13 195 HC Deb. col 584–6.
14 Ibid., col 787.
15 Ibid., col 862–4.
16 *National Sailors' and Firemen's Union of Great Britain* v. *Reed* [1926]
    Ch. 536; for discussion and further references, see 42 *Law Quarterly Review* (1926), pp. 289, 295, 296.
17 [1911] AC 179.
18 [1915] AC 120.
19 Cmd 4060.
20 See above, p. 12.
21 The standard work on housing during this period is M. Bowley,
    Housing and the State 1919–1944 (1945).
22 See above, p. 3.
23 See especially W.R. Garside, *British Unemployment 1919–1939* (1990).
24 Ibid., pp. 343–5.
25 Cmd 3937, p. 99.
26 *R. v. Minister of Health ex parte Davis* [1929] 1 KB 619.
27 *R. v. Minister of Health ex parte Yaffe* [1930] 2 KB 98.
28 [1931] AC 494; see W.I. Jennings 'Courts and Administrative Law'
    in 49 *Harvard Law Review* (1936), p. 426.
29 See speech of Minister of Health (A. Greenwood) introducing the
    Housing Bill 1930: 237 HC Deb. col 1806–7 (7 April 1930).
30 *In re Bowman* [1932] 2 KB 621.

31 Cmd 3937, App. V.
32 Cmd 4372, p. 89.
33 Report by F.C.S. Bradbury MD, DPH, appointed by National Association for Combating Tuberculosis, cited in Ellen Wilkinson, *The Town That Was Murdered* (1939), pp. 240–4.
34 Wilkinson, *The Town That Was Murdered* (1939), pp. 191–2.
35 PRO HLG 11/25.
36 *Errington* v. *Minister of Health* [1935] 1 KB 249.
37 [1911] AC 179 (see above, p. 15).
38 [1935] 1 KB 286.
39 [1936] 1 KB 40.
40 See below, p. 52.
41 *Prescott* v. *Birmingham Corporation* [1955] Ch. 210.
42 *Bromley* v. *GLC* [1983] 1 AC 768; see below, pp. 154–7.
43 See below, Ch. 3.

2 Wartime and reconstruction

Imprisonment without trial

Modern warfare demands total commitment. A government must be able, when necessary, to take control of the country's assets including manpower and property. Direction of labour will be necessary as will requisition of property. Legal powers must be taken for these purposes.

In 1939 the overriding legal instrument was the Emergency Powers (Defence) Act. This authorized His Majesty in Council to make such regulations as appeared to him to be necessary or expedient for securing the public safety, the defence of the realm, the maintenance of public order and the efficient prosecution of the war, or for maintaining supplies and services essential to the life of the community. The wording was purposely wide to ensure both that regulations could be made to cover every eventuality and that their legality would be difficult to challenge in the courts.

The Emergency Powers (Defence) Act was enacted on 24 August 1939. On 25 August and 1 September, Defence Regulations were made under the authority of that Act. Regulation 18B empowered the Secretary of State for the Home Department to make an order detaining any named person without trial. Such detention was, no doubt, a huge invasion of personal liberty, justifiable only by the emergency. The British declaration of war against Germany was made at 11 a.m. on 3 September.

As first drafted the Regulation provided that the Secretary of State could make a detention order, if satisfied that it was necessary to do so.[1]

Regulations made under Order in Council or otherwise by Ministers, under statutory authority, normally are laid before the Houses of Parliament which may either be required to approve them or be enabled to annul this draft of them. On 31 October 1939, Dingle Foot MP moved to annul Regulation 18B, amongst others. 'The main function of this House nowadays', he said rather forlornly, 'is to watch and pray.' Sir John Anderson was Home Secretary and his responses to criticism of the width and vagueness of the Regulation were punctuated by interruptions from other Members. The columns of Hansard show that he had a hard time of it and he was forced to agree to consult further with a view to introducing an amended version. On this understanding the motion to annul was withdrawn.

The consultation took the form of an informal conference at which the Home Office was represented by the Home Secretary, the Parliamentary Under-Secretary, the Principal Private Secretary to the Home Secretary and the Permanent Under-Secretary; there also attended the First Parliamentary Counsel (the senior draftsman) and two or possibly three Conservative, three Labour and three Liberal MPs.

The new Regulation 18B which was substituted for the earlier version came into force on 23 November 1939. It provided:

> If the Secretary of State has reasonable cause to believe any person to be of hostile origin or associations or to have been recently concerned in acts prejudicial to the public safety or the defence of the realm or in the preparation or instigation of such acts and that by reason thereof it is necessary to exercise control over him, he may make an order against that person directing that he be detained.

In addition the Home Secretary had power, under the royal prerogative and without statutory authority, to detain the nationals of any country with which the United Kingdom was at war. Many such 'enemy aliens' were taken into custody, most being Jewish and other refugees from Nazi Germany. Regulation 18B was directed primarily at British subjects who were thought to present actual or potential risks to national security.

After eight months, the war burst into general activity when on 10 May 1940 the Germany armies invaded Holland and Belgium. Between 27 May and 3 June, the British army, with many French troops, altogether a total of some 338,000 men, retreated via Dunkirk to England. Later in June, a further 220,000 were brought back from other ports. On 22 June France concluded an armistice with Germany.

These events gave rise to fears, based in part on rumours of Germany infiltration into Holland and Belgium before the attack, of spies and traitors. Some 30,000 enemy aliens were rounded up. British subjects detained under Regulation 18B numbered 1,428 at the end of August 1940. Altogether 1,847 orders under the Regulation were made during the war but the number in detention began to fall in 1941. There were only 266 in detention under the Regulation at the end of 1943, sixty-five at the end of 1944, and eleven at the end of the war in Europe in May 1945.

The detailed categories of these persons are not known but the largest single group of some 750 seems to have been members or former members of the British Union of Fascists founded in 1932 by Sir Oswald Mosley (who was detained with his wife until 1943). Another 550–600 were of Italian descent. Some members of the Irish Republican Army were also interned. No full list of names was published.

As we have seen, each order for detention was made by the Home Secretary who was Sir John Anderson until Herbert Morrison succeeded him in October 1940. The Home Secretary acted on the recommendation of MI5 (part of the security services) or the police who effected the arrest. Each case was then passed to an Advisory Committee chaired throughout the war by Norman Birkett who was appointed to a High Court judgeship in November 1941. Detainees had the right to object to detention and the chairman of the Committee was required to give information of the grounds on which an order had been made and to furnish detainees with such particulars as were in the opinion of the chairman sufficient to enable them to present their case. These grounds and particulars were contained in a document called 'Reasons for Order' which, however, gave the detainees no information about the evidence on which they were being held.

The Advisory Committee examined detainees on the basis of a much more detailed document called 'Statement of the Case', compiled by MI5 after the order had been made. It did not necessarily include all the grounds on which the Home Secretary had made the order.

Originally it had been proposed that detainees could be represented before the committee by lawyers but this was dropped. Birkett said later:

> The Committee was satisfied that the absence of legal assistance placed the appellant in no real disability, for they regarded it as a duty to assist the appellant to formulate and express the answers he or she desired to make.

It may be doubted whether all the detainees shared this view. Witnesses against the detainee (whether from M15 or elsewhere) were rarely heard by the Committee, and never in the presence of the detainee. Birkett also stated that his Committee worked on the principle that if any doubt remained it was to be resolved against the detainee.

After examining the detainee, the Advisory Committee made its recommendation for or against continuing the detention to the Home Office which under Sir John Anderson accepted their view in every case. Under Herbert Morrison, the department, headed by Sir Alexander Maxwell as Permanent Under-Secretary, occasionally disagreed with the recommendation, both continuing the detention of some recommended for release and (very much less often) releasing some not so recommended. From 1941, cases were reviewed annually. But there were also special reviews in individual cases and some policy decisions which resulted in group releases. In a few instances – for example for Mosley – the War Cabinet was involved. These decisions to review and to release (or not) appear to have been taken mainly by officials, sometimes, but not often, after reconsideration by the Advisory Committee.

Although, because of the terms of the Emergency Powers (Defence) Act 1939, it was effectively impossible to challenge in the courts the validity of Defence Regulations, it was possible to argue that the exercise of a power in a particular case exceeded the terms of the Regulations.

Eleven days after the Defence Regulations were promulgated by Order in Council on 1 September 1939, Robert William Liversidge applied for a commission in the Royal Air Force Volunteer Reserve and was later assigned to administration and special duties, including intelligence. In his application he claimed to have been born in Toronto in 1901 of Canadian parents. In fact, he was born in the United Kingdom in 1904 as Jacob Perlsweig, son of a Russian rabbi emigré. He changed his name to Liversidge in 1937.

The RAF police placed him under close arrest on 26 April 1940 (when he was working at Fighter Command headquarters) because of his earlier misstatements about his personal history. Then on 28 May he was detained under Regulation 18B on the ground of having 'hostile associations'. The story is not clear. The case against him may have originated with the Metropolitan Police in London who informed MI5. But MI5 seem not to have directly sought his detention themselves. On 2 October, 'Reasons for Order' were supplied to his lawyers. They included references to his false statements, said he was associated with swindlers and crooks, and also from time to time 'with Germans and with those associated with the German Secret Service'. Liversidge's lawyers asked for details of this last ground (which was the only information about 'hostile associations') but were refused. The Advisory Committee found the ground 'really difficult to substantiate' nor were they impressed by the other grounds. Nevertheless they recommended detention which the Home Secretary accepted on 10 December 1940. Liversidge was confined in Brixton prison until released on 31 December 1941.

What association (if any) Liversidge ever had with the German Secret Service is not known, though it is possible that some of his business activities in peacetime could have brought him into touch with military and political intelligence. This may explain the reluctance of MI5 directly to secure his arrest. There is no evidence to suggest that he was not a loyal subject or that he was a security risk. The Advisory Committee, which saw him again before his release, made clear that he was a person in whom confidence could be placed.

Liversidge decided to challenge the legal validity of his arrest and detention and began an action against the Home Secretary for damages for false imprisonment. Regulation 18B as we have seen began with the words 'If the Secretary of State has reasonable cause to believe' and Liversidge applied for particulars of the grounds of this belief. He argued that the words of the Regulation required the Home Secretary to have a cause that was 'reasonable'; that the words did not provide that the Home Secretary was to be the only judge of the reasonableness of the cause; that therefore the test of the reasonableness was objective, determinable by a court; and that before a court could come to its determination it must know what were the particular grounds on which the Home Secretary had decided that he had reasonable cause to believe.

We have seen that the first version of the Regulation required the Home Secretary only to be 'satisfied . . . that it was necessary' for him to make an order to prevent action prejudicial to the public safety or the defence of the realm. Some of those involved in the consultations in 1939 may have thought that the new words opened the Home Secretary to challenge in the courts. Sir William Jowitt conceded as much as Solicitor-General in arguing the first case to arise under the regulation, *in re Lees*,[2] whilst contending that a court had no right to see confidential material. Whether the Home Secretary's decision could be reviewed by the courts was the question that divided the Appellate Committee of the House of Lords in *Liversidge* v. *Anderson*.[3] In effect Jowitt's concession was denied.

The case was argued on 18, 19 and 22 September 1941 and their Lordships' speeches were delivered on 3 November 1941. The war was not going well. The strategic air offensive was resulting in heavy losses of bombers and their crews to very little advantage; Germany's invasion of the Soviet Union, launched on 22 June, was still progressing; in North Africa, the British army was on the defensive; the Japanese were threatening Malaya, the Dutch East Indies and Singapore.

The five Law Lords who heard the case were Lords Maugham, Atkin, Macmillan, Wright and Romer. All except Atkin were agreed that Liversidge's request that the Home Secretary disclose his grounds for detention must be denied and that his decision could not be reviewed by the courts. In support of this they advanced a number of reasons. The most general was exemplified by Lord Maugham:

> It seems to me reasonably clear that if the thing to be believed in is something which is essentially within the knowledge of A.B. or one for the exercise of his exclusive discretion, the words might well mean if A.B. acting on what he thinks is reasonable cause (and, of course, acting in good faith) believes the thing in question.

But their main concern was to protect the Executive. Their other reasons included the confidential nature of the information justifying the detention and its non-disclosure in court or elsewhere, what Lord Wright called the 'dire national peril' of the times, the Minister's responsibility to Parliament, the existence of the advisory committees, and the inappropriateness of the courts for review of matters of this kind.

Of the four Law Lords forming the majority, Maugham was the most senior. He had made his own way at the Bar. In 1928 he was appointed as a Chancery judge, promoted to the Court of Appeal in 1934, and to the House of Lords the next year. In 1938 he became Lord Chancellor for eighteen months and sat again as a Law Lord from 1939 to 1941. He was seventy-five years of age at the time of *Liversidge* v. *Anderson*. He had little political experience and on the evidence of his autobiography was by nature a reactionary of the most bigoted kind.[4] He held strong views on the need for the judiciary to be independent of the executive and, on the evidence of his judgment in *Liversidge*, on the need for the executive to be independent of the judiciary.

Macmillan had some political experience, having been a Unionist candidate for Parliament before serving in the Labour Government of Ramsay MacDonald as Lord Advocate in 1934. In 1930 he was appointed directly to the House of Lords without prior judicial experience. In 1939–40 he was Minister of Information. Then he returned as a Law Lord until 1947. His support of the executive in *Liversidge* was wholly in keeping with his 'independent' political position.

With Wright we move onto the high plane of truly distinguished judges. He was a judge from 1925 to 1947, being a Law

Lord from 1932 to 1935, the Master of the Rolls 1935 to 1937 and a Law Lord again from 1937 to 1947. He and Atkin were the two most influential senior judges from the early 1930s until the end of the war.

Romer was a Chancery judge from 1922 to 1929, then promoted to the Court of Appeal and appointed a Law Lord in 1938 until his retirement in 1944.

Atkin was alone in the minority and his dissent has become famous. Like Maugham he was near the end of his career. He was first appointed as a judge in 1913, sat in the Court of Appeal from 1919 to 1928 and was a Law Lord from 1928 to 1944. Future historians may call him the greatest British judge in the first half of the twentieth century. We have already noted his judgment in *R. v. Roberts*.[5]

In *Liversidge* Atkin argued that the test of the reasonableness of the Home Secretary's 'cause to believe' must be something which could be challenged in the courts, that the standard was one to be objectively determined, not to be wholly left to the Home Secretary's discretion.

The often quoted passage in his judgment must be set out in full:

I view with apprehension the attitude of judges who on a mere question of construction when face to face with claims involving the liberty of the subject show themselves more executive minded than the executive. Their function is to give words their natural meaning, not, perhaps, in war time leaning towards liberty, but following the dictum of Pollock C.B. in *Bowditch* v. *Balchin*, cited with approval by my noble and learned friend Lord Wright in *Barnard* v. *Gorman*: 'In a case in which the liberty of the subject is concerned, we cannot go beyond the natural construction of the statute'. In this country, amid the clash of arms, the laws are not silent. They may be changed, but they speak the same language in war as in peace. It has always been one of the pillars of freedom, one of the principles of liberty for which on recent authority we are now fighting, that the judges are no respecters of persons and stand between the subject and any attempted encroachments on his liberty by the executive, alert to see that any coercive action is justified in law. In this case I have listened to arguments which might have been addressed acceptably to the Court of King's Bench in the time of Charles I.

I protest, even if I do it alone, against a strained construction put on words with the effect of giving an uncontrolled power of imprisonment to the minister. To recapitulate: The words have only one meaning. They are used with that meaning in statements of the common law and in statutes. They have never been used in the same sense now imputed to them. They are used in Defence Regulations in the natural meaning, and, when it is intended to express the meaning now imputed to them, different and apt words are used in the regulations generally and in this regulation in particular. Even if it were relevant, which it is not, there is no absurdity or no such degree of public mischief as would lead to a non-natural construction. I know of only one authority which might justify the suggested method of construction: 'When I use a word', Humpty Dumpty said in a rather scornful tone, 'it means just what I choose it to mean, neither more nor less'. 'The question is', said Alice, 'whether you can make words mean so many different things.' 'The question is', said Humpty Dumpty, 'which is to be master – that's all.' (*Through the Looking Glass*, c.vi). After all this long discussion the question is whether the words 'If a man has' can mean 'If a man thinks he has'. I am of opinion that they cannot, and that the case should be decided accordingly.

This was fighting talk and his biographer tells us that he knew he had not spared his colleagues. 'I hope', he said, 'that I shall be on speaking terms afterwards.'[6] His hope was not to be wholly realized.

Lord Simon was Lord Chancellor and he saw a copy of Atkin's judgment a few days before it was delivered on 3 November 1941. He wrote to Atkin about the 'very amusing citation from Lewis Carroll', but wondered if it was 'necessary'. It might be 'wounding' and, with a fine example of reverse double-speak, felt that 'neither the dignity of the House, nor the collaboration of colleagues, nor the force of your reasoning would suffer from the omission' of the quotation. Atkin was unmoved.

Lord Caldecote was Lord Chief Justice and he was shocked by the attack on judges and 'the effect upon the reputation of the Bench for impartiality already produced by your words'. Atkin denied there was any criticism of judges generally or imputation of subservience to the executive.

The strongest reaction came a few days later when Lord Maugham took the extraordinary though very English step of writing a letter to the editor of *The Times*. He was particularly incensed by Atkin's reference to counsel's arguments being likened to those that might have been addressed acceptably to the King's Bench in the time of Charles I. Counsel, said Lord Maugham, could not reply 'even to so grave an animadversion' as this, but he had heard nothing in their arguments that could justify such a remark.

This was heavy artillery ponderously wheeled into position and laboriously fired. Atkin thought Maugham must be 'suffering from nervous strain'. A question was put down in the House of Lords inviting the Lord Chancellor to reprove Lord Maugham for writing his letter and Maugham made a statement in the House which ended by inviting Atkin to say that he did not intend to comment adversely on the conduct of counsel. But Atkin remained silent throughout the whole of this charade.

The objections taken to Atkin's speech centred on the 'Alice' quotation and the comment on the arguments advanced by counsel for the Crown, that is for the Home Secretary. Atkin accepted, in his reply to Lord Simon's letter, that the reference to Humpty Dumpty was meant to ridicule the method by which his colleagues reached the construction they put on the words 'If the Secretary of State has reasonable cause to believe'. It could be said that Atkin departed from the convention that judicial disagreement with other members of the court should be phrased in the most decorous language. But Atkin was deeply moved by the issue as he saw it. If the Government was to take the fundamental power to imprison citizens without trial then the terms of that power had to be strictly adhered to and not extended. Once the principle of giving words their natural meaning was departed from in such a case, the function of the judiciary was subverted.

Lord Maugham's complaint, that to attack the arguments advanced by counsel was unfair because they could not reply to 'so grave an animadversion', was trivial. It is always understood that the job of counsel is to put forward propositions in support of their case and that, unless they act dishonestly, their personal reputation is not remotely involved. And the idea that the Attorney-General needed the protection offered by Lord Maugham is absurd and would, one supposes, have been rejected by Sir Donald Somervell himself.

Atkin's plain speaking certainly divided public opinion, with some supporting both his conclusions and his language, while others disagreed. But subsequently, judicial opinion came down forcefully on his side. In 1950, Lord Radcliffe for the Judicial Committee of the Privy Council (which is composed largely of Law Lords hearing appeals from overseas territories) said, 'It would be a very unfortunate thing if the decision of *Liversidge's* case came to be regarded as laying down any general rule as to the construction of such phrases.'[7]

Finally, in a case where the statutory powers were similarly phrased, officers of the Inland Revenue seized and removed papers. It was conceded that the officers had to show that 'in fact' they had reasonable cause. Lord Scarman said:

> The ghost of *Liversidge* v. *Anderson* therefore casts no shadow on this statute. And I would think it need no longer haunt the law. . . . It is now beyond recall.[8]

While this is no doubt true of the argument on the proper interpretation of words empowering public authorities to act if they have 'reasonable cause', opinions may still differ on whether the majority or Atkin came to the proper conclusion in the circumstances of the case itself in 1941. Later, Wright said:

> The strength of the Government's case lay largely in the provision of the Regulations for an advisory committee which was established under the presidency of so powerful a judge as Mr Justice Birkett. It is true that the Committee's powers were advisory and did not bind the secretary [of state] to obey them or even involve them, but that, with the whole context of the Regulation and the circumstances of the time, was held sufficient to justify a construction of the Regulation in the sense claimed by the Government and thus to legalize the man's detention.[9]

Atkin was not famous as a great champion of the individual versus the state. On the judicial role in the interpretation of statutes he was not in the rigid conformist tradition, and was prepared to look for Parliamentary intention and purpose. But he was concerned, like Lord Greene (as we shall see), to keep distinct the functions of the judiciary and the executive and to stand for the independence of the former. This may have been the strongest motive for his dissent in *Liversidge* where his judgment reads, in part, as written in anger and protest at the assumption that the judges would support the executive in a matter of this kind and at such a time. Perhaps, like Dingle Foot in another institution (see above, p. 37), he feared that the effect of government by Defence Regulations was to reduce the judiciary to do no more than 'watch and pray'. And in *Liversidge* he did not play the game according to the established rules. Atkin's background[10] was very different from that of English judges and he never seems to have fitted easily into the traditional stereotype. He was the oldest of three sons of an Irish father and Welsh mother who emigrated to Australia in 1864 to a sheep-farming station in Queensland where Atkin was born in 1867. His father soon abandoned sheep-farming, became a journalist and a Member of the Queensland legislature but died in 1872 at the age of thirty. Atkin's mother returned to her native Wales in Merioneth with her three sons. In 1878, Atkin attended school at Christ College Brecon whence he won a classical demyship to Magdalen College Oxford in 1885. After graduating he was called to the Bar. As we have seen, he was appointed to be a judge in the King's Bench Division in 1913 at the age of forty-five.

Liversidge v. *Anderson* demonstrates one judicial characteristic above others. As a retired Law Lord put it to me: 'the judges are a patriotic bunch'. In the end, as many instances show, political considerations take precedence over those of individual rights and freedoms. This is particularly so when national security is invoked. The danger is that threats to the state are so widely drawn, so easily asserted, and so imprecise that they swallow up individual rights whose claims to attention at this level must rest on principle. Mr Liversidge, however admirable, could not as an individual expect to be treated more generously than others. What mattered was the principle because if that were disregarded for him it could be disregarded in very many other like cases.[11]

Post-war problems

During the second half of the 1930s, and in the immediate post-war period, the courts followed the principles laid down in *Errington* to govern the rights of objectors to compulsory purchase and clearance orders, and to appeals to the Minister from the refusal of local planning authorities to grant permission for the development of land. As we have seen, although *Errington* and the other cases put certain restrictions on Ministers in their relations with local authorities in order to protect those rights, attempts to widen these restrictions so as to prevent prior consultation between the two groups of public authorities, or to require full disclosure of their dealings with one another, were unsuccessful. We may say that in the 1930s the attitude of the courts to the exercise of statutory powers was not antagonistic. The courts did not like the interference with private property rights explicit in much legislation relating to housing, public health and the control of land use. But once their decisions in the early cases (especially *ex parte Davis*) were reversed by legislation, they put up no consistent resistance.

Many problems faced the Labour Government when it took office in July 1945. Most commodities were in short supply, much devastation had been caused by air-raids. Many wartime regulations were retained and the Government began to take powers to establish the post-war welfare state and to bring basic industries under national control. Some fears expressed about the attitude of the judiciary to the introduction of Labour policies proved to be unfounded. In the event there was relatively little scope for judicial intervention, and it is doubtful whether the judges had much inclination to seek to limit Governmental activities as conducted by the Attlee administration. The need for strong government was obvious and, at least for the first two years, there was little opposition in the country despite the general austerity. The principles of a planned economy were similar to those which had applied throughout the war years when the vast majority of the adult population had been in the armed forces or working in civil employment under government direction.[12]

The nationalization of basic industries, controlled by public corporations with Ministers formally kept at arms' length, did not give rise to litigation and the compensation paid to former shareholders was generous. The National Health Service and the new Social Security provisions diverted to administrative tribunals conflicts which might have found their way to the courts. The only provisions which did become litigious were, not surprisingly, those which interfered with property rights. Town and country planning legislation empowered Ministers and local authorities to exercise control over the development of land and its use. Conditions were attached to the grant of planning permission and these, being restrictive and so reducing the value of property, were contested. But the courts mostly limited themselves to ensuring that conditions were not imposed for purposes other than those for which, in the judicial view, they were given and in particular took a realistic view of the nature of the administrative process and of the relationship between central and local authorities. The courts tended to support these planning conditions, giving the benefit of the doubt to the Minister and the local authorities. Their upholding of an exercise by a governmental body – the Central Land Board – of compulsory purchase to enforce a sale of land at existing use value was, nevertheless, surprising.[13]

Judicial decisions in four cases of 1947 reflected the attitude of the courts. The first concerned an area of Plymouth which had been heavily bombed. The statute provided that where the Minister was 'satisfied that it is requisite' for the purpose of dealing satisfactorily with extensive war damage, that land should be laid out afresh and redeveloped as a whole he could make a compulsory purchase order after holding a local inquiry at which objection by property owners would be heard.[14] The objection was that as the borough council proposed to retain the existing fronts of certain houses and rebuild them, the Minister could not be so satisfied. But the Court of Appeal (Lord Greene MR presiding) strongly upheld the wide discretion given to the Minister by the words of the statute. The Court refused to go behind the expression by the Minister of his satisfaction that it was requisite he should act as he did. No doubt those words do not give the Minister absolute power. He must act honestly and in good faith. But the court would not substitute their own judgment for his. Moreover, the Minister was not obliged to act only on the evidence presented at the local inquiry. He could make his own unfettered policy decision.

This approach was upheld by the House of Lords in a different situation a few weeks later on 24 July. Here the statute empowered the Minister to make an order designating an area as the site of a new town. He was required to be 'satisfied that it is expedient in the national interest' for him to do so, after the holding of a public local inquiry.[15] The new town was Stevenage and, even before the Bill which gave the Minister his powers was passed by Parliament, he addressed a public meeting in the area at which he made clear his intention to press ahead with the building of this new town designed to relieve the pressure on London by providing housing and business accommodation. When his order was made it was challenged on the ground that his speech showed 'bias', in that he had forejudged any genuine consideration of objections or had not seriously considered them. But Lord Thankerton dismissed this, saying that no judicial or quasi-judicial duty was imposed on the Minister and that his duties were purely administrative. Lord Thankerton was not saying that any irregularities in procedure, had such been shown, at the local inquiry or elsewhere, were irrelevant. He was saying that the Minister was required to have a policy and entitled to carry it out.

Heuston tells us that this case caused Lord Chancellor Jowitt 'some personal embarrassment' and that he was 'careful not to preside' over the hearing of the appeal to the House of Lords from the decision of the Court of Appeal that the Minister had acted impartially. Heuston says that the Law Lords went even further than the Court of Appeal in the direction of abdicating judicial control over administrative action but that in 1948 the courts 'were anxious not to seem to hinder the social legislation of the Attlee Government'.[16] I suspect that Lord Thankerton would have been surprised to hear his speech so interpreted.

The decision in *B. Johnson & Co. (Builders) Ltd.* v. *Minister of*

Health[17] in the Court of Appeal (Lord Greene MR again presiding) was handed down on the same day. This concerned a compulsory purchase order for housing purposes and letters written by the local authority to the Minister before the draft order was made public. The contents of these letters were not disclosed to the objectors to the order. Lord Greene emphasized that the Minister's functions were 'fundamentally administrative', subject only to the qualification that, in respect of his obligation to consider objections made to the order, a quasi-judicial duty was superimposed to hear both sides fairly. One of the letters referred to the objectors as speculative builders, which they said was derogatory and might have affected the way the Minister considered their objections. But Lord Greene took the narrower view of the quasi-judicial obligation of the Minister and held that there was no need for him to disclose the letters because they related to the administrative function of the Minister in coming to his policy decision. He said:

> It is obvious to anyone who has any familiarity with the operations of government departments that matters of high public policy, such as this, are or may be, under constant consideration and review by the necessary minister. The problem does not, so to speak, arrive suddenly out of the blue by the putting forward by the local authority of a compulsory purchase order for confirmation. The housing conditions in great cities are the subject of continuous consideration, not merely by one ministry, but by several. Information may have arrived, reports may have been obtained, representations and arguments may have been put forward by other ministries, and in a great many cases one would expect to find a fairly bulky file. . . . It is not unfair to say that, generally speaking, the idea that a minister can be compelled to disclose to anybody information of that kind, which he has obtained as a purely administrative person, is alien to our whole conception of government in this country. . . . There is no single case in the books where it has been said, or indeed, suggested, that the obligation of the Minister in considering objections, as regards discovery [that is, disclosure], goes beyond an obligation to see that matter which has come into existence for the purpose of the quasi-*lis* is made available to both sides, and *I am not going to extend the obligation on the Minister beyond that point* (emphasis added).

While this formulation in no way conflicts with the decision in *Errington*[18] the application of the principles laid down in the 1930s favours the administrative authorities.

Finally in this group of 1947 decisions came one that was over the years to be cited in innumerable subsequent cases. The *Wednesbury* decision[19] handed down by Lord Greene MR in the Court of Appeal in November did not become seminal and produce progeny immediately but, as fashions changed, it began paradoxically to be cited as an authority not for the legal rule which determined the outcome but for the so-called principles which it enunciated by the way. The legal rule was in favour of the public authority and supported the exercise of its discretionary power. But Lord Greene was forced by the logic of his own argument to admit certain hypothetical exceptions and these have subsequently been used as one basis of the profound change in judicial attitudes that was to come several years later. It was a case that had nothing to do with post-war planning.

The Sunday Entertainments Act 1932 legalized the opening of cinemas on Sundays subject to such conditions as the licensing authority – in this case, the council of the borough of Wednesbury – thought fit to impose. The council imposed this condition: 'No children under the age of fifteen years shall be admitted to any entertainment, whether accompanied by an adult or not.' This last phrase relates to a former Board of Film Censors rule, adopted by licensing authorities that, for what were then called 'A' films, children had to be so accompanied. In my childhood, we used to stand by the box office clutching our sixpence (or whatever it was) and accost any adult stranger with the question: 'Will you take me in please?' Generally the adult silently agreed, took the money, paid, and in we walked, immediately separating and going to different seats. Everyone knew it was a farce which it was in no one's interest to upset.

In Wednesbury, cinema proprietors protested at the condition on the ground that it was unreasonable. The statutory power was obviously very widely drafted, like that in the *Poplar* case,[20] and seemed on its face to give to the local authority an absolute discretion to impose any conditions whatsoever. Had the condition excluded children with red hair it would, on a literal interpretation, have fallen within the statutory words. But, as we have seen, the courts have never taken so literal a view. They have looked at the context in which the words are used and have limited the exercise of the discretion to that context. So, since the colour of a child's hair could have no relevance to its attendance or non-attendance at a cinema on a Sunday, the courts would certainly have declared the imposition of such a condition to be beyond the powers of the authority. I have chosen an absurd example but problems about relevance will obviously arise on the margin. How should the courts decide whether such a condition is or is not valid?

Lord Greene set out his propositions as follows. First, the courts could interfere only if it were shown that the authority had contravened the law. Second, the burden of establishing that proposition was on those who asserted it. Third, the court must not substitute itself for that authority and was not a court of appeal. Fourth, the court could set aside the exercise of the authority's discretion only when one or more of the following principles was infringed. If, in the statute conferring the discretion, there were to be found expressly or by implication matters which the authority ought to have regard to, then it must have regard to those matters. Conversely, if it appeared that certain matters would not be germane, then the authority must not have regard to those matters. More generally, the authority must not act in bad faith or dishonestly. And the authority must not act 'unreasonably'.

It is this last ground that has caused much of the subsequent difficulty. As Lord Greene said, 'unreasonableness', as a phrase, was often used comprehensively and could then include having regard to irrelevant matters and absurdity (like my example of the child with red hair). But he said that counsel for the plaintiffs was using unreasonableness as an independent ground for attacking the decision of the authority. At first, Lord Greene rejected this, saying:

> Once it is conceded, as it must be conceded in this case, that the particular subject-matter dealt with by this condition was one which it was competent for the authority to consider, there, in my opinion, is an end of the case. Once that is granted, [counsel for the

appellants] is bound to say that the decision of the [local] authority is wrong because it is unreasonable, and in saying that he is really saying that the ultimate arbiter of what is and is not reasonable is the court and not the local authority.

And that was unacceptable. But then Lord Greene admitted another possibility: 'It is true to say that, if a decision on a competent matter is so unreasonable that no reasonable authority could ever come to it, then the courts can interfere. That, I think, is quite right; but to prove a case of that kind would require something overwhelming, and, in this case, the facts do not come anywhere near anything of that kind.' The local authority's condition was upheld. Lord Greene's view was close to that of Atkin and Scrutton in *Roberts* v. *Hopwood*.[21]

The interest of this case is that it seeks to define the grounds on which a court can and cannot properly exercise control over the discretionary powers of public authorities; and it also indicates the grey areas where the grounds are uncertain. But the main thrust of the argument is that a court has only limited rights to interfere, that Parliament has given these powers to those authorities and a court should not substitute its view for that of the authorities. This approach was wholly in accordance with Greene's political philosophy.

One case stood midway in time between *Roberts* v. *Hopwood* (1925) which we have discussed above and *R.* v. *GLC ex parte Bromley* (1981) which we shall discuss below. This concerned, as they did, the use of ratepayers' money. Birmingham City ran a bus service and decided to provide free travel during limited periods for women over sixty-five and men over seventy years of age at an annual cost of £90,000 to be met out of the general rate fund. The Court of Appeal (Lord Evershed MR, Jenkins and Birkett L JJ) held that the City owed a fiduciary duty to the ratepayers which was breached by this scheme. The City were obliged 'to operate their transport undertaking substantially on business lines' and 'misapprehended the nature and scope of the discretion conferred on them and mistakenly supposed that it enabled them to confer benefits in the shape of rights of free travel, on any class or classes of the local inhabitants appearing to them to be deserving of such benefits by reason of their advanced age and limited means'. This singular decision[22] threatened the validity of ninety-six such concessionary schemes and had to be reversed by legislation.[23] It seems that such modest exercises in municipal enterprise continuously raise the spectre of encroaching socialism in the minds of the judiciary.

Wilfred Arthur Greene had a brilliant career at Oxford and was elected a Fellow of All Souls in 1907. He had a war record of much distinction and became hugely successful at the Chancery Bar. He was appointed directly to the Court of Appeal in 1935, being Master of the Rolls from 1937 to 1949, then to the House of Lords very briefly before he died in 1952. His influence during those years was strong. Greene is often regarded as a highly conservative judge who took a most restricted view of the judicial function. But his position was more subtle than that.

In 1938 Greene delivered the presidential address to the Holdsworth Club on 'The Judicial Office'. He saw the judiciary very much as an institution existing alongside the other two great bodies: Parliament and the executive. The rules of public policy which the courts had elaborated he called 'an excrescence on the law'. They were the proper concern of Parliament, not the courts. He strengthened this argument by reference to the 'totalitarian' societies of the USSR and Germany where judges were 'nothing more nor less' than instruments of the executive.

No doubt Lord Greene was a conservative by temperament. But his views were clearly influenced, as were those of many of his generation, by the First World War and by the international and political events of the 1930s. In 1944, he delivered a lecture on 'Law and Progress'[24] where he developed a part of the earlier theme. Here he used the metaphor of a democratic 'machine' having three elements: the legislative, the administrative, and the judicial. The machine was an 'integral whole', having 'essential unity' and a 'single purpose'. Judges, he said, should not 'depart from the language used by Parliament in order to produce what may appear to them a juster result or one which they may think Parliament would have intended if its attention had been drawn to the point. . . . Policy is not the concern of judges save in so far as the manifest objects of the statute, as appearing on its face, may provide a context pointing to one interpretation rather than another.'

The lesson which Lord Greene might have been expected to draw from his condemnation of judicial subordination in totalitarian regimes was to emphasize the importance of judicial independence of the executive in order to protect the individual from the overweening power of the state. That is the conventional conclusion for those who see conflict in society as primarily between private persons and public authorities. But Lord Greene's emphasis is quite different. He separates the three 'elements' – the legislative, the administrative, and the judicial – and he is at pains to insist that, in particular, judges should not use their power of interpretation to improve on statutory provisions or to become involved in matters of policy. To that extent he could be classed with the literalist judges whom Lord Denning, amongst others, was to criticize. But Greene's special vision is to see the three constitutional institutions as being the elements of one machine serving a single purpose. The separateness of the judiciary is functional, not part of some system of checks and balances. He does not see the judiciary as having the duty to impose its own standards of behaviour on the executive. Greene's corporatism depends not on conscious collusion between the three elements but on their mutual recognition of the single purpose they serve. If we seek to define this purpose we shall get no nearer than saying it is the continuation of the government of the country along the lines already laid down, though extended and changed over the years. The purpose is conservative and evolutionary, maintaining the basic structure of society and the relationship between classes within the economy. Ministers of the Crown, Parliamentarians and judges have distinct functions within the one machine but all work together towards a common end. Like all forms of corporatism the image is somewhat alarming.

For all Greene's rejection of judicial creativity or even of modest interpretations which seek to reflect what Parliament might have had in mind, he is inevitably driven into subjectivism of some sort. In the *Wednesbury* doctrine who but judges can decide what is relevant and what is not, when improper use of statutory power slides into bad faith, what are the acceptable and the unacceptable limits of unreasonableness? Even when judges are as anxious as Lord Greene to keep judicial review within strict limits, they retain some ultimate discretion to restrain the exercise of executive power when, in their opinion, it is in the common interest that they should do so. That 'public policy' which Greene so condemned as an excrescence on the law reappears as blemishes on the fair skin of the judicial body.

Greene's general philosophy was distinct from that of the conceptualists. He did not share their antagonism to the executive. He took a realistic view of the necessary workings of Government departments and especially of the final authority of Ministers to decide matters of policy. This does not mean that during his tenure as Master of the Rolls, Ministers were given a free hand. But the Court of Appeal certainly did not seek to find ways in which the decisions of public authorities could be overturned. And the Law Lords played a less prominent role during the second half of the 1940s than they had played before or were to play in the future.

When the Conservative party returned to office in 1951 it was widely expected that David Maxwell Fyfe (later Lord Kilmuir) would be appointed Lord Chancellor by Churchill. But the Prime Minister wanted him in the House of Commons as Home Secretary. To the surprise of most people (and certainly to his own) Gavin Simonds, who had been a Law Lord since 1944, was appointed. Churchill whom, Simonds recorded, 'I had met but who did not remember meeting me',[25] was looking for a stop gap. Simonds's background had been entirely in the law. He had been a High Court judge from 1937 until his elevation in 1944 and had no political experience at all except as a member of the Committee on Ministers' Powers[26] where, said another member, 'He did not make any great contribution to our discussions, nor did the quality of his observations justify the portentousness of his manner'.[27] Kilmuir said that he 'was innocent of politics as a newly baptised babe and obviously enjoyed his immersion enormously'.[28]

Unlike Greene, Simonds believed in judicial passivity when interpreting statutes. In 1949 he clashed (not for the last time) with Lord Justice Denning, newly appointed to the Court of Appeal. In a case the facts of which are unimportant Denning said:

A judge, believing himself to be fettered by the supposed rule that he must look to the language and nothing else, laments that the draftsmen have not provided for this or that, or have been guilty of some or other ambiguity. . . . When a defect appears a judge cannot simply fold his hands and blame the draftsman. He must set to work on the constructive task of finding the intention of Parliament and he must do this not only from the language of the statute, but also from consideration of the social conditions which gave rise to it, and of the mischief which it was passed to remedy, and then he must supplement the written word so as to give 'force and life' to the intention of the legislature.[29]

Two years later, Denning LJ repeated his doctrine:

We do not sit here to pull the language of Parliament and of Ministers to pieces and make nonsense of it. That is an easy thing to do, and it is a thing to which lawyers are too often prone. We sit here to find out the intention of Parliament and of Ministers and carry it out, and we do this better by filling in the gaps and making sense of the enactment than by opening it up to destructive analysis.

This aroused the wrath of Lord Simonds when the case went on appeal.[30] He said that the general proposition that it was the duty of the court to find out the intention of Parliament and of Ministers could not by any means be supported. And of the proposition that the court should fill in the gaps, he said:

It appears to me to be a naked usurpation of the legislative function under the thin guise of interpretation. And it is the less justifiable when it is guesswork with what material the legislature would, if it had discovered the gap, have filled it in. If a gap is disclosed, the remedy lies in an amending Act.

The reluctance of the courts to interfere was shown strikingly in two very different cases. In *Nakkuda Ali* v. *Jayaratne* the Controller of Textiles in Ceylon cancelled a license under powers which enabled him to do so where he had reasonable grounds to believe that a dealer was unfit to be allowed to continue as such. The Judicial Committee of the Privy Council in an opinion

delivered by Lord Radcliffe held that the Controller was not acting judicially but was 'taking executive action to withdraw a
privilege'. So the dealer was unable to challenge the decision although he alleged that there were grave falsifications in the books
of a branch of the Controller's office.[31]

Smith v. *East Elloe*, decided in 1956, is sometimes cited as
the highest point in this literal approach to statutory words. Despite the general acquiescence of the courts, the executive tried to
make assurance doubly sure by statutory provisions limiting their
jurisdiction. The Act of Parliament which authorized compulsory
purchase of land for statutory purposes allowed challenge in the
High Court to the validity of a compulsory purchase order made
by a local authority within six weeks of its confirmation by the
Minister. The Act then provided that otherwise 'a compulsory
purchase order . . . shall not . . . be questioned in any legal proceedings whatsoever'.

Land belonging to the appellant having been made the subject
of an order, she brought an action nearly six years later against
the local authority, the clerk to the local authority, and the Minister,
claiming a declaration that the order was invalid because it had
been made and confirmed wrongfully and in bad faith and that
the clerk had acted wrongfully and in bad faith.[32]

The fact that the appellant had failed to begin her action within
the statutory six weeks seemed to bring her within the exclusionary
clause and so to prevent her from bringing any action. But the
appellant's allegation, in part, was that she was the victim of bad
faith (akin to fraud) which she could not have detected within six
weeks. This being so it would not have been surprising had the
Law Lords held that the exclusionary clause could not have been
intended to prevent the action going forward. They did agree
that the action against the clerk for damages could proceed but by
a majority of three to two they held that the exclusionary clause
ousted the jurisdiction of the court to hear the actions against the
local authority and the Minister.

In the majority, Viscount Simonds expressed little sympathy
for the exclusionary clause but 'it is our plain duty to give the
words of an Act their proper meaning and, for my part, I find it
quite impossible to quality the words of the paragraph. . . . What

is abundantly clear is that words are used which are wide enough to cover any kind of challenge.' Lords Morton and Radcliffe agreed in similar terms.

It is significant for the future change in judicial attitudes that Lord Reid dissented. He said that the exclusionary clause:

> is clearly intended to exclude, and does exclude entirely, all cases of misuse of power in *bona fide*. But does it also exclude the small minority of cases where deliberate dishonesty, corruption or malice is involved? In every class of case that I can think of the courts have always held that general words are not to be read as enabling a deliberate wrongdoer to take advantage of his own dishonesty. Are the principles of statutory construction so rigid that these general words must be so read here? Of course, if there were any other indications in the statute of such an intention beyond the mere generality of the words that would be conclusive: but I can find none.

Lord Somervell, also in the minority, said of the exclusionary clause: 'If Parliament had intended that this should apply in the case of a person defrauded it would have made it plain, and not left it to be derived from a doubtful syllogism.'

In 1954, Simonds was somewhat summarily required to resign as Lord Chancellor to make way for Lord Kilmuir. Simonds was immediately appointed as a Law Lord and remained a powerful influence until 1962.

Simonds's passivity in the interpretation of statutes did not go unchallenged. Apart from Reid, Somervell dissented in a number of cases. Like Reid, Somervell had a political background having been a Conservative MP from 1931 to 1945, Solicitor-General 1933–6, Attorney-General 1936–45 (when he was counsel for the Crown in *Liversidge* v. *Anderson*, as we have seen) and briefly Home Secretary in 1945. From 1946 to 1954, Somervell was a Lord Justice in the Court of Appeal and from 1954 to 1960 a Law Lord. Also serving alongside Simonds from 1949 to 1964 was another formidable figure: Lord Radcliffe, who had been Director-General of the Ministry of Information from 1941 to 1945. His influence on governmental matters was considerable, both as chairman of commissions and committees into taxation and the monetary system and of numerous inquiries into national security and the public service. He was widely admired in some quarters, and in others as widely disliked. Of the Simonds era he said: 'It is only in quite recent times that the vitality of the judicial contribution to statute law seems to have declined into a patient exposition of the apparent.'[33]

Simonds is an example of a judge of much intellectual ability who prefers to stay clear of 'political' questions by pretending they do not exist. This he is able to do by adopting a literal approach to the words of statues. Judges with political experience are in danger of empathizing too closely with Ministers and administrators. The best judges use their political experience to inform but not dominate their judgment.

Retrospect

The wartime cases, of which *Liversidge* was the most dramatic, present the conflict between the maintenance of rules designed to prevent the arbitrary use of power and the need, in a national emergency, to act speedily and drastically and to invade rights not only of property but of personal freedom. It is perhaps more, not less, necessary in wartime to use extraordinary powers in a principled manner. This happened when the House of Commons forced reconsideration and amendment of Regulation 18B as first drafted. And the key words in Atkin's dissent were that there was 'no such degree of public mischief as would lead to a non-natural construction'. That is to say, it was not *necessary* to adopt the interpretation preferred by the majority. Therefore it was necessary not to adopt it. Lord Wright's defence that there were administrative safeguards – the procedure of the Advisory Committee – does not touch the point of principle. If it could have been shown that the adoption of Atkin's interpretation might well have led to loss of life by requiring the state to disclose its grounds for the detention of suspects (which could conceivably have been helpful to the enemy) then, in wartime, the abandonment of the principle of adopting the natural construction of the words might have been justified. But had the Law Lords gone along with Atkin, the

Government could, if it wished, have asked Parliament to approve an amended Regulation. And that would have preserved the principle as the rules made by Parliament override the interpretation adopted by the courts.

The case was and is important as it illustrates the basic rule that accepted principles should never be abandoned because it is thought to be expedient to do so. The case is an extreme example because of the circumstances of war. But it is out of extremities that such rules can be fully tested. The Law Lords bent the principle of interpretation to fit the needs of the time, as they saw those needs. But, in so doing, they adopted the dangerous axiom referred to by Atkin: *silent enim leges inter arma.*

No such dilemmas faced the judges during the late forties and the fifties. For the first six years under the Labour Governments, times were hard but many radical changes were sought to be introduced. In *The British Economy since 1945* Cairncross lists under six headings: the controls used by Government: prices; consumer rationing; investment; raw materials allocations; import restrictions; and to some extent controls over the employment of labour. None of these gave rise to significant litigation. In the regulation of land use and the attempts, largely unsuccessful, to tax increases in development values, the courts, as we have seen, gave governments a relatively free hand. The cases of *Robinson*, *Franklin* and *Johnson* reflected the reluctance of the courts to interfere with the exercise by public authorities of their statutory powers in the post-war period of reconstruction. They led to the statements of principle laid down by Lord Greene MR in the *Wednesbury* case. As we have seen, this decision, though it reads as if delivered extempore and not as a reserved judgment, pulls together, in a principled way, the grounds of judicial review and strikes a particular balance between the executive and the courts.

It has been suggested that perhaps the judges wanted to make clear how radical and dangerous, in peacetime, the changes were. But this is too conspiratorial and too sinister an interpretation. It must be remembered that during the post-war years, well into the 1950s, it was believed that planning could prevent a return to the social evils of the 1930s. And indeed the controls did ensure a fairer distribution of scarce commodities resulting, for example, in major house-building programmes, and the National Health Service. The sceptics, which may have included many of the senior judiciary, withdrew to the sidelines. Attlee's Lord Chancellor Jowitt was no socialist and only a Labour man on sufferance, but he certainly had nothing to gain by rocking the political boat. When Churchill selected Simonds as his first post-war Lord Chancellor he expected little and would have been alarmed had he had more. And when after 1954 Simonds continued as the senior Law Lord his passivity, though it departed from Greene's much more active principles, fitted well enough with the judicial spirit of the times. But perhaps Lords Reid, Radcliffe and MacDermott chafed under it.

Then Kilmuir as the new Lord Chancellor became deeply involved in the Suez affair enmeshing law and politics.

Notes

1 For much of what follows, see A.W.B. Simpson, 'Rhetoric, Reality and Regulation 18B' (The Child and Co Oxford Lecture 1987); also his 'Detention without Trial in the Second World War' (16 Florida State University Law Review 225, 1988); and 'The Judges and the Vigilant State' (Child and Co Lecture 1989). These articles have now been overtaken by his *In the Highest Degree Odious: Detention with Trial in Wartime Britain* (1992). I am much indebted to the author for allowing me to draw on this material and for his personal advice and help.

2 [1941] 1 KB 72; 57 TLR 26, 68.

3 [1942] AC 206; and see *Greene* v. *Secretary of State for Home Affairs* [1942] AC 284. See generally Geoffrey Lewis, *Lord Atkin* (1983); R.F.V. Heuston in 87 *Law Quarterly Review* (1971), p. 161 and 86 *Law Quarterly Review* (1970), p. 33.

4 See F.H. Maugham, *At the End of the Day* (1954), pp. 565–6; and Stevens, *Law and Politics: The House of Lords as a Judicial Body 1800–1976* (1979), pp. 243–4.

5 See above, pp. 6–7.

6 G. Lewis, Lord Atkin (1983), p. 138.

7 *Nakkuda Ali* v. *Jayaratne* [1951] AC 66 at 77; see above, pp. 58–9.

8 *IRC* v. *Rossminster* [1980] 1 All ER 80 at 104.

9   Wright, 'Lord Atkin of Aberdovey', in 32 *Proceedings of the British Academy* (1946), p. 307.

10   See G. Lewis, note 6 above, pp. 1–27.

11   See the *Hosenball* case, below, pp. 123–6.

12   See Cairncross, *The British Economy since 1945* (1992), Ch. 2, and his *Years of Recovery* (1985).

13   *Earl Fitzwilliam's Wentworth Estates Co.* v. *Minister of Housing and Local Government* [1952] AC 362. Denning LJ dissented in the Court of Appeal [1951] 2 KB 284.

14   *Robinson* v. *Minister of Town and Country Planning* [1947] KB 702.

15   *Franklin* v. *Minister of Town and Country Planning* [1948] AC 87.

16   Heuston, *Lives of the Lord Chancellors 1940–1970* (1987), p. 109.

17   [1947] 2 All ER 395.

18   See above, pp. 28–9.

19   *Associated Provincial Picture Houses Ltd.* v. *Wednesbury Corporation* [1948] 1 KB 223.

20   See above, p. 5.

21   See above, pp. 6–7.

22   *Prescott* v. *Birmingham Corporation* [1955] Ch. 210.

23   Public Service Vehicles (Travel Concessions) Act 1955 and 537 HC Deb. col 756 (18 February 1955).

24   94 *Law Journal*, pp. 349, 357, 365.

25   Heuston, *Lives of the Lord Chancellors 1940–1970* (1987), p. 148.

26   See above, pp. 16–17.

27   See note 25 above, p. 144.

28   Kilmuir, *Political Adventure* (1964), p. 194.

29   *Seaford Court Estates* v. *Asher* [1949] 2 KB 481.

30   *Magor and St Mellons RDC* v. *Newport Corporation* [1952] AC 189.

31   [1951] AC 66.

32   *Smith* v. *East Elloe Rural District Council* [1956] AC 736.

33   'Law and the Democratic State' (Holdsworth lecture, 1955)

3 Suez and the lawyers

The Lord High Chancellor of Great Britain has, as all first-year law students know, three main roles.[1] He is a member of the Cabinet, the head of the judiciary, and the Speaker of the House of Lords. In his first role, he must be a supporter of the Government of the day; in his second, he must be a distinguished lawyer; in his third role, he must be reasonably competent in chairmanship of a large and diverse body. He is said to be chief legal adviser to the Government but the more objective and technical advice comes from the Attorney-General (or the Lord Advocate for Scottish matters) who has also many independent and statutory duties. In Cabinet the Lord Chancellor is the person whose legal advice may be sought and his considered opinion is always available to the Prime Minister and the Cabinet during a continuing crisis, sometimes to the alarm of the other Government lawyers.[2] To the outside world, he is the principal lawyer in Government and his views carry great weight. He is seen as responsible for the administration of justice and for its reform. Formally the Lord Chancellor presides over all the judicial activities of the House of Lords, including the appellate committees when the Law Lords hear argument and deliver judgment in a case before them. But since the 1950s the Lord Chancellor has sat infrequently and in his absence one of two senior Law Lords, specifically named as Deputy Speakers for judicial purposes, presides.

The confusion of the roles of the Lord Chancellor was vividly demonstrated in the Suez affair. In 1854 the Turkish Viceroy, having suzerainty over Egypt, authorized the formation of a company to construct the Suez Canal, with a concession to last ninety-nine years from the date of its opening. Thereafter, unless alternative arrangements were made, the Canal was to pass to the Egyptian Government. Despite strong British opposition at first, the Canal was opened on 17 November 1869. Subsequently, Arab threats and violence in Egypt resulted in the Turkish Viceroy in 1880 inviting the UK Government to station troops at key points along the Canal – a 'temporary occupation' which lasted for seventy-four years. In 1888 a Convention was signed by the United Kingdom, France, Germany, Austria-Hungary, Italy, Russia, Spain, Turkey and the Netherlands, article 4 of which recited that the Canal should always be 'free and open, in time of war as in time of peace, to every vessel of commerce or of war, without distinction of flag'. However, in 1950, as a result of border conflicts between Egypt and Israel, Egypt prohibited ships bound for Israel from using the Canal and this was countenanced by other nations. In the mid 1950s, the Suez Canal Company had thirty two directors of whom sixteen were French, nine British (including three representatives of the UK Government which was the Company's most important shareholder), five Egyptian, one Dutch and one from the USA. The Egyptian Government took 7 per cent of the Company's gross profits.

In the early 1950s, there had been demonstrations led by the Muslim Brotherhood against the British presence in Egypt. Attacks were made on property owned by the British and other foreigners and there were some deaths, including those of the British Council representative and the Canadian trade representative. A group of young Egyptian army officers staged a coup against King Farouk, who abdicated in July 1952, and in March 1953 General Neguib became President. In April 1954, Colonel Nasser, leader of the young officers, became Prime Minister and the effective leader of the country. In October 1954, Anthony Eden became British Foreign Secretary, and negotiated an Anglo-Egyptian treaty under which the British troops were to leave the Canal zone, an operation completed in June 1956.[3]

For several years there been border conflicts between Israel on the one hand and Egypt and Jordan on the other, with many deaths. A particular raid on Egyptian camps in Gaza at the end of

February 1955 resulted in the deaths of thirty-six Egyptian and Palestinian soldiers and two civilians. Kyle says that 'For Nasser it changed everything' and 'the overriding need was to ensure Egyptian rearmament from whatever sources it could be obtained'.[4]

The Soviet Union was ready to supply this need as part of its policy to support Arab causes in the Middle East. The western powers became greatly alarmed, especially as by this time the UK Government was hoping to enlist Egypt's support in seeking a solution to the problems of the Palestine refugees and of relations with Israel generally.

In addition the Soviet Union indicated its willingness to help with the finances needed to build a large dam on the Nile at Aswan in upper Egypt. Anthony Eden had succeeded Winston Churchill as Prime Minister in April 1955, and for a while during that year it seemed that the western nations, including the USA, would be willing to help finance the dam if this would keep out the Soviet Union. In December a World Bank loan was offered with grants from the British and American Governments.

Early in 1956, Eden became more and more convinced that Nasser was dangerous and aggressive, as well as pro-Soviet, and saw parallels with the western 'appeasement' of Hitler and Mussolini in the 1930s. Then at the beginning of March 1956, General Sir John Glubb, who had long been employed by the King of Jordan as commander of the Arab Legion, was dismissed and Eden saw the hand of Nasser in this. On 8 March, Eden's Secretary noted, 'Today both we and the Americans really gave up hope of Nasser and began to look around for means of destroying him.'[5]

On 19 July 1956, the USA withdrew its support for the Aswan dam and a week later Nasser announced the nationalization of the Suez Canal.

There followed a period of intense diplomatic activity. In 1950, the USA, Britain and France had issued a statement, commonly referred to as the Tripartite Declaration, which recognized that Israel and the Arab states needed to maintain a certain level of armed forces but which declared their 'unalterable opposition to the use of force or the threat of force'. The three powers stated that if they found any state was preparing to violate frontiers or armistice lines they would immediately take action 'both within and outside the United Nations' to prevent such violation. In practice the three powers kept under joint scrutiny requests for arms from any of the states in the region.

The USA was, in any event, bound to be involved in international developments in so crucial an area as the Middle East but, led by President Eisenhower and Secretary of State Foster Dulles, was also strongly committed to the United Nations and reluctant to use force against Egypt. The British and the French eventually, and fatally, decided to make their own plans without telling the USA.

Some pretext was necessary if military action was to be taken against Egypt to bring about the fall of Nasser. Various possibilities were discussed by the British, the French and the Israelis. But Scott Lucas concludes that, by mid October, Eden's resolve for military action had disappeared. This he bases on a cable sent by Eden to the Foreign Secretary (Selwyn Lloyd) who was in New York on 14 October, suggesting that negotiations should be opened with the Egyptian Government. This cable was despatched at 11.30 p.m. Ninety minutes later two envoys brought a proposal from the French Prime Minister asking Eden what action Britain would take if Israel attacked Egypt. Scott Lucas argues that Eden's immediate priority was to prevent British involvement in what looked like an imminent outbreak of hostilities between Israel and Jordan. If this had happened, Jordan would then have invoked the Anglo-Jordanian treaty of 1948 and called on the United Kingdom to support him, with the result that Eden's policies in the eastern Mediterranean would have collapsed.[6] At least it can be said that this was an additional reason for Eden to embrace the French plan.

Two meetings were held in great secrecy at Sèvres, a suburb of Paris on 22 and 24 October 1956. It was agreed that Israel would launch a large-scale attack on Egypt on the evening of 29 October 'with the aim of reaching the Canal Zone the following day'. Then, 'on being apprised of these events', the Governments of Britain and France would issue two separate and simultaneous 'appeals' to the belligerents (Israel and Egypt) to stop all military action and to withdraw all their forces, in the case of Israel 10 miles to the east of the Canal and in the case of Egypt to the west of the Canal. As the main Israeli army would be between 50 and 100 miles east of the Canal at the time when the ultimatum was issued, the Israelis could advance 40 to 90 miles and still comply. But Egypt was also to be required to accept 'the temporary occupation of key positions on the Canal by Anglo-French forces to guarantee freedom of passage through the Canal by vessels of all nations until a final arrangement'. If either Israel or Egypt rejected the appeal or failed to give its agreement within twelve hours, the Anglo-French forces would take the necessary measures. The conditions imposed on Egypt were intended to ensure that Egypt would reject the 'appeal'. The Anglo-French attack against the Egyptian forces would be launched early on 31 October. As Ben-Gurion, Israel's Prime Minister, noted in his diary on 17 October: 'The English propose that we should start on our own, they will protest, and when we reach the Canal they will come in as if to separate and then they'll destroy Nasser.'[7]

The Israeli attack on Egypt would thus be the pretext on which Anglo-French forces could pretend to be intervening to separate the combatants. The intended result of the operations was the establishment of the Anglo-French forces on the Canal, with the Israelis also deep in Egyptian territory.

The terms of this plan were intended to be secret for all time. Indeed Eden was dismayed when told that they had been committed to paper and sought, unsuccessfully, to have all copies destroyed. Only a few members of the British Cabinet knew of the collusion with Israel and France. Eisenhower and Dulles were told nothing because it was believed they would not have consented to any such course of action.

On 29 October, Israeli forces entered Egypt and paratroops were dropped some 20 miles east of Suez. On 30 October, the ultimatums, with a twelve-hour limit on compliance, were presented to Israel and Egypt. Eden told Eisenhower there was a case for saying Israel had acted in self-defence but added: 'Nevertheless we would not wish to support or even condone the action of Israel', a statement which in the history even of international affairs must take a high place for hypocrisy. Eisenhower immediately dissociated himself from the Anglo-French ultimatums and in the Security Council the USA called for a complete withdrawal of Israeli forces and a ceasefire. This resolution and another in similar terms were vetoed by Britain and France, who on the evening of 31 October dropped bombs on Cairo. On 5 and 6 November, British forces landed at Port Fuad and occupied part of the Canal zone and further bombing caused military and civilian casualties.

It seems that the British Government believed that the Government of the USA would, when the critical point was reached, support the United Kingdom, despite the disapproval of the use of force expressed by President Eisenhower and others. As early as 8 August, the Permanent Secretary to the UK Treasury warned that action would place Britain's balance of payments and foreign reserves under considerable pressure and on 7 September stressed the need for maximum support from the USA.[8] In the event the USA reacted strongly against the invasion and in the General Assembly of the United Nations, early on 2 November, Britain was condemned by sixty-four votes to five and labelled an aggressor. At home, opinion was sharply divided. Under financial pressure from the USA, positively obstructing British efforts to protect sterling by drawing on the International Monetary Fund, and refusing to implement plans for diverting oil supplies to Britain, and also under a Soviet threat of intervention, the UK Government on 8 November declared a ceasefire and was soon forced to accept a withdrawal in favour of a United Nations force, having achieved none of its purposes and having suffered a major disaster. The Suez Canal passed fully into Egyptian management.

Two legal questions arose out of these events. The first was whether Nasser had acted illegally in nationalizing the Canal. The Cabinet minute of 27 July 1956 reads:

> The Cabinet next considered the legal position and the basis on which we could sustain, and justify to international opinion, a refusal to accept the decision of the Egyptian Prime Minister, Colonel Nasser, to nationalise the Canal.
>
> The Cabinet agreed that we should be on weak ground in basing our resistance on the narrow argument that Colonel Nasser had acted illegally. The Suez Canal Company was registered as an Egyptian company under Egyptian law; and Colonel Nasser had indicated that he intended to compensate the shareholders at

ruling market prices. From a narrow legal point of view, his action amounted to no more than a decision to buying out the shareholders. Our case must be presented on wider international grounds. Our argument must be that the Canal was an important international asset and facility, and that Egypt could not be allowed to exploit it for a purely internal purpose. . . . The Canal was a vital link between the East and West and its importance as an international waterway, recognised in the Convention signed in 1888, had increased with the development of the oil industry and the dependence of the world on oil supplies. It was not a piece of Egyptian property but an international asset of the highest importance and it should be managed as an international trust.[9]

On that day Eden sent a telegram to President Eisenhower saying: 'We should not allow ourselves to become involved in legal quibbles about the rights of the Egyptian Government to nationalize what is technically an Egyptian company or in financial arguments about their capacity to pay the compensation which they have offered. . . . My colleagues and I are convinced that we must be ready, in the last resort, to use force to bring Nasser to his senses.'[10] Nevertheless on 1 August the Lord Chancellor (Kilmuir), the law officers and the legal adviser to the Foreign Office produced a paper seeking to prove that Egypt had acted illegally. This listed the threat of force to keep British and French subjects working at the Canal; this threat showed that Egypt was unable to operate the Canal, in breach of the Convention of 1888; this Convention had been entered into on the basis of a company operated by Britain and France; the company had acquired an international character; an eminent international lawyer had supported this view from which Egypt had not dissented; to nationalize such a company was a breach of international law.[11] Eden's biographer comments that this was 'very thin gruel'.[12] The Convention had said nothing about the ownership of the Canal and Nasser's action did not violate the provision in the Convention that passage should not be impeded.

The second question was whether the armed intervention by Britain and France could be justified under international law. On this, the Attorney-General (Sir R. Manningham-Buller), as senior law officer in the Government, and the legal adviser to the

Foreign Office (Sir Gerald Fitzmaurice), differed sharply from the Lord Chancellor. From the beginning Lord Kilmuir had been in favour of the use of force if need be. In mid October, Scott Lucas tells us that Eden allowed Anthony Nutting (Minister of State at the Foreign Office) to inform two of his colleagues of the crucial state of events created by the French plan but objected to the briefing of Sir Gerald saying, 'That's the last person I want consulted. The lawyers are always against our doing anything. For God's sake keep them out of it. This is a political affair.'[13] On 1 November the Attorney-General wrote to the Foreign Secretary: 'On what is known to me, I am unable to devise an argument which could purport to justify in international law either our demand that [Egypt] who had in no way threatened our nationals, should withdraw her forces from a part of her own territory which she is engaged in defending or the threat to occupy her territory by armed forces should she fail to accede to that demand.'[14]

On the same day Lord Kilmuir spoke in Parliament in the opposite direction. As we have seen, he had been Lord Chancellor since 1954, having served his time in the Home Office. He had been a Conservative MP since 1935, becoming Solicitor-General in 1942. He made his name at the Nuremburg trials in 1945, prosecuting the surviving German leaders for war crimes (and other offences). After the general election in that year, he was most active on the Opposition benches and, working in collaboration with R.A. Butler, presented the report on Conservative party organization in 1948–9. From 1951 to 1954 he was Home Secretary. During his eight years as Lord Chancellor (1954–62) he sat as a judge on only twenty-four appeals[15] and, says Heuston, left the disposition of appeals 'to the Chancery Law Lords (Simonds, Radcliffe, Morton, Cohen and Jenkins) who were predominant at the end of the fifties.'[16]

Throughout the Suez crisis, Kilmuir supported Eden with, when necessary, legal opinions to justify the Prime Minister's policy. Kilmuir argued[17] that the Government, in invading Egypt, was 'completely justified' in law. Force, he said, might lawfully be used or threatened, under the Charter of the United Nations, either with the express authority of the Security Council or in self-defence. Article 51 of the Charter provides:

> Nothing in the present Charter shall impair the inherent right of individual or collective self-defence if an armed attack occurs against a Member of the United Nations, until the Security Council has taken the measures necessary to maintain international peace and security.

Lord Kilmuir took strength from a letter published in *The Times* on 11 August from Professor Goodhart, a distinguished academic lawyer and Master of University College Oxford. The Professor's letter was somewhat oblique: 'The claim to absolute territorial sovereignty is especially unwarranted as the argument that there can be no restrictions on a State in regard to its own territory has no foundation . . . the doctrine of territorial sovereignty does not entitle a State to disregard its international obligations . . . there can be no doubt that in fact the Suez company has always been international.' But it was clearly intended to suggest that the use of force was not limited to repelling a direct attack and so could support an invasion.

At the meeting of the Egypt Committee of the Cabinet on 4 September, Eden said that it was important the public should be fully informed of the legal case in support of the action proposed to be taken. It would, he said, be 'helpful if other eminent members of the legal profession could be induced to set out their views in columns of the responsible press'. The Committee invited the Minister of Defence and the President of the Board of Trade to consult with the Lord Chancellor with a view to securing this.[18]

Lord Kilmuir argued that a state might properly use force to protect a vital national interest which had been imperilled; and in such a case the state which had altered the status quo was guilty of aggression.[19] Kilmuir argued that self-defence undoubtedly included a situation in which the lives of a state's nationals abroad were threatened and it was necessary to intervene on that territory for their protection. He continued that the test of whether such intervention was necessary under customary international law was, first, whether there was an imminent danger of injury to nationals; secondly, whether there was a failure or inability on the part of the territorial Sovereign to protect the nationals in question; and, thirdly, whether the measures of protection of the intervener were strictly confined to the object of protecting these nationals against injury. As there had been no threat to the lives or persons of British nationals the Lord Chancellor had to extend his justification. 'It has been argued', he said, 'that there is a great distinction between the protection of human lives and the protection of property'. This was not a proposition to which he gave 'absolute concurrence'.

> I take the view that if really valuable and internationally important foreign property is in danger of irreparable injury, through the breakdown of order, entry by a foreign State for the sole purpose of securing the safety of that property is excusable.

Kilmuir could not argue that the Canal was British property so he had to argue that the invasion was 'excusable' to protect foreign (that is, Egyptian) property because it was 'really valuable' and 'internationally important'. I take the view, he continued:

> that, since we can show that the blocking of or interference with the Canal for a considerable period would cause ... irreparable damage and suffering to a number of nations, for which it would be difficult to see adequate compensation being afforded, our intervention is also justified by the danger to the Canal.

So he found 'three good grounds of intervention': the danger to British nationals; the danger to shipping in the Canal; and the danger to the enormously valuable installations of the Canal itself.

Lord Kilmuir argued that the Charter of the United Nations did not cut down the customary right of forceable self-defence by restricting it to cases where the attack provoking it had actually been launched. In other words there could be preventive self-defence taken before the opponent had delivered the first blow. This begins to look like a general excuse for aggression and caused the Archbishop of Canterbury (Geoffrey Fisher) to intervene and ask, 'My Lords, the noble and learned Viscount referred to the attacking Power against which we have to exercise self-defence. Who is the attacking Power?' The Lord Chancellor replied that self-defence extended to the protection of our nationals and continued:

> first, we make a peaceful landing; then, if the Power into whose territory we are going says that they will resist with all their force, the force which we have the right to use is automatically extended to that sufficient to repulse the force threatened.

Which, then, repeated the Archbishop, is the attacking Power in this case? Kilmuir replied 'the person who threatens to use force in answer to a proffered peaceful intervention. . . . The threat of force is made by the person who refuses to stop the hostile operations that are threatening the people and the installations.' The Archbishop asked again, 'Who is the attacking Power in this case?' and received the answer: 'I should have thought the most reverend Primate might have guessed that for himself. It is obviously Egypt, who has refused to stop.' The Archbishop suggested that Israel was the attacking force. But, said the Lord Chancellor, there were two situations:

> There is the first situation, which attracted our peacemaking intention, which was started when Israel crossed the border. Then there is the second situation . . . when the Egyptians refused our peaceful measures.

The Archbishop had the last word: 'I merely said there are two stages, one and two. You omitted the first. I have now inserted it'.

It is difficult to believe that Lord Kilmuir was unaware of the conspiracy involving the Governments of Israel, France and the United Kingdom, although he claimed in the debate that the motives of Her Majesty's Government were not being questioned in the House. Lord Blake believed that the Cabinet was fully informed on 25 October about Sèvres and the measures that were about to be taken.[20] Kilmuir must surely have known that his claims to the 'peacemaking intention' and 'peaceful measures' of the UK

Government were ill-founded and that the purpose of the invasion was to replace Nasser with a leader more sympathetic to Israel, French and British interests.

However, it must be said that in his autobiography, Lord Kilmuir stated:

> The wild accusations of collusion between the British, French and Israeli Governments which were hurled by the Labour Party had absolutely no foundation in fact. Far from eagerly seeking an excuse to occupy the Canal for our own purposes of doing to Nasser what we had been unable to do in August, we strove to avert a situation in which military intervention was necessary.[21]

But, this apart, the legal arguments were very weak. Kyle tells us that the Attorney-General, the Solicitor-General and the legal adviser to the Foreign Office had not been asked about the Government's proposal to use force and would not have supported it.[22] It was impossible to see, said that legal adviser, how the policy could be justified merely on the basis of an Egyptian refusal to clear out of a large zone of their own territory in face of Israeli attacks. The plea of vital interests was the very one which the UN Charter intended to exclude as a basis for armed intervention. Protection of one's citizens applied only when the local government had lost control. Neither British citizens nor British property were endangered by Egyptian action.

Similarly Lord McNair, recently retired as President of the International Court of Justice, who had been prepared to argue for the illegality of the nationalization of the Canal, wholly opposed the use of force saying he was unable to see the legal justification of the threat or the use of armed force by Great Britain against Egypt in order to impose a solution of the dispute.[23] The former Lord Chancellor Jowitt expressed the same view.[24]

Retrospect

Politicians who are set on a course of action they believe to be popular are seldom deterred by arguments based on allegations of illegality. They know that if the action is believed to be necessary and is successful they will not be condemned merely because they contravene some rule of law. On the other hand if the course of action is controversial and the illegality blatant, they will hesitate to pursue that course where the risk of failure is real. The price to be paid may be too high if the opponents to the policy are give the card of illegality to play. If the illegality is not blatant or its discovery thought to be improbable then the risk may be taken.

Breach of domestic law – statute or the common law – is easily challengeable once it is known, and the courts are open for this purpose. But successful challenge will not be easy, especially if the judges conclude that the action is being brought for party political reasons rather than for the establishing of a legal right or the award of compensation. But the bringing of the action itself may be important for the making of a political point.

Breach of international law is politically less dangerous. The interpretation of the rules is more open to dispute and their enforcement much more difficult. Indeed, a sovereign state may refuse to accept the judgment of an international court – as happened when the USA was found guilty of breaching its obligations by intervening in the affairs of Nicaragua in 1986 – and no remedy is available. But where the support of allies is sought in some international venture, the illegality of what is proposed may provide a valid reason (or an excuse) for non-co-operation.

The Anglo-French plot, intended to provide a legal pretext for the invasion of Egypt in 1956, was designed to bring the action within Article 51 of the UN Charter. This, it was hoped, would placate world opinion and, in particular, encourage the President of the USA to support or, at worst, not oppose the military action. On one version of the events, Eden seems to have been reluctant to invade if no pretext could be found. Perhaps he thought that this would be more than Eisenhower could stand. But, being provided with a legal pretext, Eden may have decided that Eisenhower would not move against him. It is interesting that Eden was anxious to be seen to be acting within the law. It is more interesting that when the moment for decision came, legality was not considered to be a matter of great importance.

Notes

1   See generally on his duties (and much else) Heuston *Lives of the Lord Chancellors 1940–1970* (1987), pp. 23–31.
2   Ibid., p. 170.
3   The principal sources for the whole story are W. Scott Lucas, *Divided We Stand* (1991) and Keith Kyle, *Suez* (1991).
4   *Suez* (1991), pp. 64, 65.
5   Kyle *Suez* (1991), p. 95. In *Spycatcher* (1987) Peter Wright claimed that MI6 developed a plan to assassinate Nasser using nerve gas and that Eden at first approved it, then rescinded his approval (p. 160).
6   Scott Lucas, *Divided We Stand* (1991), pp. 228, 237; and see Robert Blake on Anthony Eden in John P. Mackintosh (ed.), *British Prime Ministers in the Twentieth Century* (1978), vol. ii.
7   Kyle *Suez* (1991), p. 298. The plan first came from the French, ibid., p. 296.
8   Scott Lucas *Divided We Stand* (1991), p. 210.
9   PRO CAB 128/30 Pt. II.
10   Sir Anthony Eden's Memoirs, *Full Circle* (1960), p. 428.
11   PRO CAB 134/1217.
12   Robert Rhodes James, *Anthony Eden* (1986), p. 479.
13   Scott Lucas, *Divided We Stand* (1991), p. 238.
14   See note 13, above, p. 274.
15   Blom-Cooper and Drewry, *Final Appeal* (1972), p. 180.
16   Heuston, *Lives of the Lord Chancellors 1940–1970* (1987), p. 175.
17   199 HL Deb. col 1347–64.
18   PRO CAB 134/1216.
19   PRO CAB 128/30 Pt. II (28 August 1956); I am indebted to Dr John Kent for drawing my attention to these CAB references.
20   R. Blake, in J.P. Mackintosh (ed.) *British Prime Ministers in the Twentieth Century* (1978), p. 102.
21   *Political Adventure* (1964), p. 278.
22   Kyle, *Suez* (1991), p. 391; see also Kyle in Wm. Roger Louis and Roger Owen (eds) *Suez 1956* (1989), pp. 114–5.
23   199 HL Deb. col 658–63 (12 September 1956).
24   199 HL Deb. col 756–62 (13 September 1956).

4 The new look of the sixties

In 1962 the attitude of the senior judiciary to the exercise of the powers of public authorities began to change dramatically. In the House of Lords this was marked by the retirement of Viscount Simonds and his replacement as senior Law Lord by Lord Reid.

James Scott Cumberland Reid was born in 1890. He was educated at Edinburgh Academy and Jesus College Cambridge where he took a First class honours degree in law. He was called to the Scottish Bar in 1914. During the First World War Reid saw active service with the Machine Gun Corps in Mesopotamia. A successful career at the Bar followed and in 1931 Reid was elected as a Unionist (Conservative) Member of Parliament for Stirling and Falkirk. At the 1935 general election, Reid was defeated but he returned to the House of Commons in 1937 as Member for Hillhead (Glasgow), a seat he held until his resignation in 1948. He gained a reputation as a formidable debater and able politician. From 1936 to 1941 he was the Scottish junior Law Officer as Solicitor-General; from 1941-4 he was the senior Law Officer as Lord Advocate. From 1945 to 1948, Reid was a front-bench Opposition spokesman in the House of Commons. In 1948 he accepted appointment as a Lord of Appeal in Ordinary (Law Lord) at the age of fifty-eight years. Reid was the senior Law Lord from 1962 until he retired in 1974, at the age of eighty-four years.

As a front-bench Opposition spokesman, records the Dictionary of National Biography, Reid 'assumed a prominent role in opposition – subjecting to penetrating and devastating criticism much proposed government legislation. He was viewed by certain

Labour politicians with hostility.' He spoke frequently and moved amendments from the Opposition front bench on the Labour Government's coal industry nationalization, emergency laws, town and country planning, exchange control, the National Health Service, new towns, agriculture, elections, housing, Crown proceedings and trade union bills.

On one occasion in 1946 Reid clashed famously with Aneurin Bevan who was Minister of Health. Reid was an Opposition member of the standing committee on the National Health Service Bill. Under clause 42 a Tribunal was to be set up to consider representations that the continuance of a particular medical or other practitioner in the service would be detrimental to its efficiency. From an adverse decision of the Tribunal, the practitioner was to have a final right of appeal to the Minister. An amendment was moved that this appeal should instead be to the High Court. Bevan opposed this on the ground that the Minister was in the position of the ultimate employer and 'we cannot admit that the courts should interpret whether the doctor has, in fact, been a good servant to the people'. This, he added 'would be real judicial sabotage of socialized services in which the functions of industrial dispute are entrusted to the judiciary'. Not surprisingly, Reid seized the political opportunity to say that the Minister had seen fit 'to charge His Majesty's judges with a desire to commit judicial sabotage on the introduction of Socialism'. Bevan replied that Reid had 'monstrously misconstrued what I said'.[1]

Lord Reid was offered the appointment to the office of Lord of Appeal in 1948 by Prime Minister Clement Attlee. There was nothing remarkable in a Labour Prime Minister appointing a Conservative barrister-politician to a judgeship, even, as in this case, to be directly a member of the highest court. While the time has passed, if it ever truly existed, for former Law Officers, to have, by convention, a claim to a judgeship, Reid, by his long experience as Solicitor-General for Scotland and Lord Advocate, and by his Deanship of the Faculty of Advocates, as well as his earlier experience at the Bar, had ample qualifications. What was somewhat unusual was for so active and prominent a member of the Opposition front bench to be so elevated.

We are told, however, that Reid himself did not jump at the

offer with immediate enthusiasm. The entry in the Dictionary of National Biography records that he first consulted the Conservative hierarchy regarding his political prospects but received no adequate encouragement.

In 1962 when Reid became the senior Law Lord, at the age of seventy-two years, a new era was inaugurated. Between 1959 and 1962, six Law Lords retired and Denning moved to the Court of Appeal. Amongst the replacements at least three (Morris, Devlin[2] and Pearce) were sympathetic to Reid's approach. Reid was in a dominant position, especially after Radcliffe and Evershed retired in 1964. The nearest in seniority was Morris and he had been appointed as recently as 1960, twelve years after Reid. Paterson says that Reid 'took a leadership role in relation to the creation of the 1966 freedom[3] as well as to how it should be exercised. He also suggested guidelines as to areas where the House should be willing to develop the law which commanded the support of a majority of his colleagues.'[4]

Two groups of cases show the radical changes that were made. The first concerned discretionary powers of public authorities; the second concerned industrial relations. These were also to be the main areas of conflict in the 1970s and 1980s.

The exercise of discretionary powers

In the five cases that follow, Reid gave the leading judgment. Eight other Law Lords participated: Morris, Hodson and Pearce in four cases; Upjohn in three; Radcliffe, Evershed, Devlin, Wilberforce and Pearson in one each. There were five dissents among the twenty-five opinions. In each case the Law Lords allowed the appeal, reversing the decision of the lower court.

The first case was about nothing more remarkable than alleged police corruption, albeit in high places.

In 1956, Ridge was appointed chief constable of Brighton police force by the local watch committee, having been a member of the force since 1925. On 25 October 1957 he was arrested and charged, with other members of the force, with conspiracy to obstruct the course of justice. On 28 October he was suspended from duty by the committee. On 28 February 1958 he was acquitted by the jury but the judge in passing sentence on two police officers who were convicted said that, on the admitted facts, neither of them had 'that professional and moral leadership' which both 'should have had and were entitled to expect from the chief constable'. On 6 March, on a charge alleging corruption against Ridge, on which no evidence was offered, the judge remarked on the need of the force for a leader 'who will be a new influence and who will set a different example from that which has lately obtained'. These were strong words indeed.

After his acquittal, Ridge applied to be reinstated but on 7 March the watch committee dismissed him. No specific charge was formulated against Ridge but the watch committee considered Ridge's statements given in evidence at the trials and the observations made by the judge. Ridge appealed to the Home Secretary who decided that there was sufficient material on which the watch committee could properly exercise their statutory power of dismissal.

Ridge brought an action against the watch committee for a declaration that his dismissal was illegal, *ultra vires*, and void and for payment of salary from 7 March or, alternatively, payment of pension from that date, and damages. The Court of Appeal held that the watch committee were taking executive action and were not bound to make an inquiry of a judicial or quasi-judicial nature and so the principles of natural justice did not apply.[5]

But the Law Lords, by a majority of four to one, held that the decision of the watch committee to dismiss Ridge was null and void, the main ground being that the committee had failed to inform Ridge of the charges against him and to give him an opportunity of being heard.[6]

The watch committee relied on the Municipal Corporations Act 1882 which empowered them to dismiss any constable whom they thought negligent in the discharge of his duty or otherwise unfit. They argued that this meant they had the executive power to dismiss even where there was a doubtful question whether a constable was guilty of a particular act of misconduct; that they were under no obligation to hear his defence before dismissing him; and that, in this case, in the light of the judge's remarks in the corruption proceedings, there was no doubt. Lord Reid concluded that the earlier authorities, mostly decided in the nineteenth century, would not have accepted this argument and would have required a hearing in accordance with the rules of natural justice. But, he said, three groups of more recent cases had apparently, in the view of the Court of Appeal in this case, justified departure from the earlier cases.

The first group consisted of those cases where Ministers, making policy decisions in the public interest, were held to be subject to the rules of natural justice only to a limited extent. The second group included wartime cases where the legislation expressly or by influence excluded those rules ('I leave out of account', said Lord Reid, 'the very peculiar decision of this House in *Liversidge* v. *Anderson*'[7]), but such cases were not of any great weight in dealing with the instant case. The third group included a much-quoted passage in a judgment of Lord Justice Atkin in 1924[8] in which he was later interpreted as having limited the application of the rules of natural justice to bodies which had 'the duty to act judicially'.[9]

The authority chiefly relied on by the Court of Appeal in holding that the watch committee were not bound to observe the principles of natural justice was *Nakkuda Ali* v. *M.F. de S. Jayaratne* discussed above.[10] Lord Reid noted that this was a decision of the Privy Council and not binding on the House of Lords. He refused to follow it.

Lord Evershed dissented. Such a matter of public notoriety, he said, required instant action by the watch committee, exercisable within the wide discretion of the statutory power. As in *Nakkuda Ali* the rules of natural justice were inapplicable to such executive action.

The importance of the majority decision of the Law Lords was that it liberated the courts from the conceptual restrictions they had created for themselves. In future, remedies would be available in many cases without the need to show that the decision complained about was judicial or quasi-judicial. It would be sufficient to show that a public authority was proceeding in a manner that was unfair.

Conflict between the executive arm of Government and the

courts could not be more direct and acute than in the second case.[11] In 1952 when the Japanese army was advancing through Burma, oil installations in Rangoon owned by the Burmah Oil Company were destroyed on the direction of the British Government. After the war the Company received £5 million by way of partial compensation and, after a further claim had been rejected by the Burma High Court in 1960, brought an action against the Crown in Scottish courts, the Company being registered there. The Company was warned by the Government that if it succeeded in its claim, legislation would be introduced to indemnify the Crown so that no money would be paid. There was no statutory power authorizing either the destruction or the payment of compensation.

In the Scottish courts the decision went first against the Government but on appeal this was reversed. The case then went to the House of Lords who by a majority of three to two upheld the claim. The majority (Lords Reid, Pearce and Upjohn) distinguished 'battle damage', for which no compensation was payable, from 'denial damage' where it was payable, and found that the destruction in this case was 'denial damage'. Lord Radcliffe strongly dissented on the ground that 'it is for those who fill and empty the public purse to decide where, by whom, on what conditions and within what limitations such compensation is to be made payable'. He was supported by Lord Hodson. The Government duly brought in its War Damage Bill, as it had promised, which was enacted despite strong protests.[12]

A similar extension of the courts' powers followed in 1967.[13] The Crown had long claimed certain prerogative powers in the interests of executive government. One of these concerned discovery of documents. This arises when, during the preliminaries to court hearing, each side requires the other to disclose relevant documents. The Crown claimed that it was entitled to refuse disclosure either of particular documents or of documents falling within a class the production of which would, in the Crown's opinion, be injurious to the public interest; and that this privilege was unchallengeable, requiring only a Minister's endorsement. In 1939, a submarine sank during its trials and ninety-nine men were drowned. Their dependents sued the shipbuilders for negligence and sought production of documents. The Crown refused on the ground that some of these documents would reveal unique features of the submarine's construction and that their public production would be of advantage to the enemy.[14] The House of Lords in that case unanimously upheld the Crown's privilege which it stated in broad terms, and made clear that the Minister's claim was to be accepted without question and without any investigation by the court.

This decision was reviewed by the Law Lords in 1967 in a case where the plaintiff was a former probationary police constable who began an action for malicious prosecution against a former superintendent of police. The plaintiff had been prosecuted for the theft of an electric torch. He was acquitted but then dismissed from his post. In the course of those proceedings various reports on the plaintiff had been made and these he sought to have produced in his action against the superintendent. The Home Secretary objected to their disclosure. He said that disclosure of confidential reports on police officers and reports concerning investigation into crime would be injurious to the public interest.

The Law Lords (Reid, Morris, Hodson, Pearce and Upjohn) on 2 May 1967 disagreed with the general principles laid down by their brethren in the earlier case.[15] They accepted that in that case the refusal to disclose the documents relating to the submarine's construction was correct but they insisted on their right to examine any documents for which Crown privilege was claimed and to decide whether or not disclosure would be injurious to the public interest. They examined the police reports and ordered their disclosure, overruling the Court of Appeal (where Lord Denning MR had dissented).

This decision was a dramatic assertion by the judiciary of their right to override the view of Minister on what was and was not in the public interest. No doubt Ministers had in the past on occasion claimed this privilege more for their own protection and that of their civil servants than because they believed the public interest would be endangered by disclosure. But it is not clear why judges rather than Ministers should have the final decision in such matters. The details of the principle are not easy to see nor did the five Law Lords who each delivered separate opinions greatly clarify the circumstances in which they believed they should review the executive powers of government. Lord Reid gave on example of a class of documents where the Ministerial decision should not be reviewed. Cabinet minutes 'and the like' ought not to be disclosed. But his reason was that disclosure

> would create or fan ill-informed or captious public or political criticism. The business of government is difficult enough as it is, and no government could contemplate with equanimity the inner working of the government machine being exposed to the gaze of those ready to criticize without adequate knowledge of the background and perhaps with some axe to grind.

Another view might be that the equanimity of governments can easily be bought at too high a cost.

A few months earlier, the Law Lords had taken even greater steps towards the curtailment of Ministerial powers. In *Padfield* v. *Minister of Agriculture Fisheries and Food*[16] a statute appeared to give the Minister a clear choice whether to act in one way or in another. But the Law Lords determined that he should have acted in the way they decided would have been appropriate.

Under the Agricultural Marketing Act 1958, the Milk Marketing Board administered a scheme by which dairy farmers sold their milk to the Board at different prices in each of eleven regions in England and Wales, the differentials reflecting the varying costs of transporting the milk from the producers to the consumers. The South Eastern Region sought to get the differentials changed in their favour by the Board. The Board consisted largely of members elected by the individual regions and any change in favour of one region would disadvantage the rest. The South Eastern Region failed to get a majority for their proposals. They then asked the Minister of Agriculture, Fisheries and Food to refer their proposal to a committee of investigation under section 19 of the Act.

Section 19 provided:

> a committee for investigation shall be charged with the duty, *if the Minister in any case so directs*, of considering and reporting to the Minister on any complaint made to the Minister as to the

operation of any scheme which, in the opinion of the Minister, could not be considered by a consumers' committee (my emphasis).

The Minister took the view that this complaint was not suitable for investigation by the committee of investigation and that the question was one for the Board to decide. So he refused the request from the South Eastern Region who resorted to the courts, asking for an order requiring the Minister to make the reference to the committee.

The Court of Appeal heard the case in July 1966. A majority (Diplock LJ and Russell LJ) held that the Minister was entitled not to refer the complaint and that this was made clear by the words 'if the Minister in any case so directs'. Lord Denning MR dissented. Rejecting the distinction between 'administrative' and 'judicial' decisions, he argued that the Minister's reasons were those which 'ought not to have weighed with him' and so he had not properly exercised his discretion. Clearly this approach is both deep and wide as it claims that the courts' authority to review the exercise of the Minister's powers extends to the evaluation of his reasons and, if they are found wanting, to set aside his decision based on them. The majority's view was essentially that the Minister's decision was one of policy for which he was accountable to Parliament, not to the courts.

The House of Lords by a majority allowed the appeal and supported the farmers. Lord Reid said:

Parliament must have conferred the discretion [on the Minister] with the intention that it should be used to promote the policy and objects of the Act; the policy and objects of the Act must be determined by construing the Act as a whole and construction is always a matter of law for the court. In a matter of this kind it is not possible to draw a hard and fast line, but if the Minister, by reason of his having misconstrued the Act or for any other reason, so uses his discretion as to thwart or run counter to the policy and objects of the Act, then our law would be very defective if persons aggrieved were not entitled to the protection of the court.

Lord Morris dissented. He said that the language of the Act as it concerned the Minister's powers was 'purely permissive' endowing the Minister with a discretion whether or not to refer the matter to the committee. It was no part of the duty of any court, said Lord Morris, 'to act as a Court of Appeal' from the Minister's decision or to express any opinion as to whether it was wise or unwise. He continued:

> A court could make an order if it were shown (a) that the Minister failed or refused to apply his mind or to consider the question whether to refer a complaint or (b) that he misinterpreted the law or proceeded on an erroneous view of the law or (c) that he based his decision on some wholly extraneous consideration or (d) that he failed to have regard to matters which he should have taken into account.

But Lord Morris found that none of these grounds existed in this case. So by a majority decision the Minister was ordered to refer the complaint to the committee which in due course recommended change. The Minister considered this recommendation but, as he was fully entitled to do, refused to accept it on the ground that it would not be in the public interest for him to do so. He referred to 'the wider questions of agricultural, economic and social policy' which were beyond the scope of the committee but which he was bound to consider.[17]

It is reasonable to assume that the legislative intention was that the Board should, as indeed Lord Reid agreed, act as an instrument for the self-government of the industry, limiting the right of the Minister to interfere only where the Board appeared to be acting contrary to the public interest. But by the same token, it is arguable that the courts should not interfere with the process unless it is clear that either the Board or the Minister has acted illegally. Here the Law Lords intervened because they thought the Minister should have exercised his discretionary powers in a particular way. That took the courts into areas of control where they had previously not presumed to go.

The fifth case arose out of the Suez affair and resulted in judgments of the Law Lords which seemed to transfer decision-making from the statutory body to which it had been entrusted and vest it in the courts.

Anisminic Ltd owned mining property in Egypt which they claimed was worth over £4 million. On the outbreak of hostilities in the autumn of 1956, the property was occupied by Israeli forces and damaged to the extent of £½ million. The property was sequestrated by the Egyptian Government on 1 November 1956 and on 29 April 1957 that Government authorized the sale of the property to an agency of the Egyptian Government, TEDO, for £½ million. Subsequently the Egyptian Government paid the UK Government £27½ million in full and final compensation for all property seized from UK owners.

It was the responsibility of the UK Government to decide who was entitled to participate in the distribution of this compensation and how much each claimant should receive. For this purpose, machinery was at hand, for in 1950 the Foreign Compensation Act had established the FC Commission. Introducing the Bill, the Minister of State had said:

> It is really more appropriate that what is essentially a judicial function of assessing claims and the shares of each different claimant should be performed now by a standing body, a judicial body, which should not merely advise the Secretary of State but actually take the decision and actually distribute the money.[18]

The chairman of the FCC is appointed by the Lord Chancellor and its members by the Secretary of State.

In 1962 an Order in Council was made under the Act of 1950, giving directions to the FCC to govern the distribution to the claimants on the Egyptian money. The Order provided that the FCC should treat a claim as established if satisfied that:

(a) the applicant is 'the owner of the property or is the successor in title of such a person'

(b) the applicant and any person who became successor in title were British nationals on 31 October 1956 and 28 February 1959.

Anisminic made a claim to the FCC which ruled against the company on the ground that its successor in title, TEDO, was not a British national. Anisminic brought an action to have this ruling set aside and Browne J found in its favour.[19] The Court of Appeal reversed this[20] but the House of Lords restored the decision of Browne J.[21]

Lord Reid explained the problem of interpretation in these words:

> The main difficulty in this case springs from the fact that the draughtsman did not state separately what conditions have to be satisfied (1) where the applicant is the original owner and (2) where the applicant claims as the successor in title of the original owner. It is clear that where the applicant is the original owner he must prove that he was a British national on the dates stated. And it is equally clear that where the applicant claims as being the original owner's successor in title he must prove that both he and the original owner were British nationals on those dates. . . . What is left in obscurity is whether the provisions with regard to successors in title have any application at all in cases where the applicant is himself the original owner.

The House of Lords decided that the interpretation put on the words of the Order by the FCC was wrong and that the applicants, being the owners of the property, did not have to prove anything with regard to successors in title whose nationality was, in these circumstances, irrelevant. The difficulty about this decision was that it had previously been thought that, when a body like the FCC was invested with the apparently exclusive right to decide, the courts could intervene only on very limited grounds. These grounds would include a positive abuse of power, or a failure to provide a fair hearing, or the taking into account of some matter which was clearly not relevant to the decision.

There was, Lord Reid said, an 'obscurity' in the meaning of the Order. But were the courts entitled to impose their interpretation over that of the FCC? One important reason why the Act of 1950 entrusted the FCC with the making of the decisions was that the distribution of the limited sum available depended on all claims being settled. If the decisions were challengeable in the courts, finality would be greatly postponed. To underline this, the Act provided that any determination by the FCC of an application 'shall not be called in question in any court of law'. The House of Lords' answer to this was that it could not apply to a determination which the courts decided was invalid and a nullity and not a real determination at all.

Lord Morris Borth-y-Gest delivered a strong dissent. As in his dissent in *Padfield* (see above, p. 86), he resisted the temptation to bend the words of the statute to enhance judicial powers. Of the FCC he said it was presumably thought that the advantages of securing finality of decision outweighed any disadvantages that might possibly result from having no appeal procedure. Of the statutory powers of the FCC, he refused to accept the sophistry required to assert, with the majority, that the FCC was acting outside its jurisdiction. He said:

If at the moment of decision they were inevitably within their jurisdiction because they were doing what they had to do, I cannot think that a later view of someone else, if it differed from theirs, could involve that they trespassed from within their jurisdiction at the moment of decision.

Lord Pearson, also dissenting, said he was not able to agree that the Commission misunderstood the Order in Council or made any error affecting their jurisdiction.

The problem then passed back to the Government and Parliament. After further dispute the Foreign Compensation Act 1969 provided that a person aggrieved by a determination of the FCC on any question of law (which includes all questions of interpretation) could require the FCC to state a case for the Court of Appeal for a final decision. This apart, no determination *or 'purported determination'* by the FCC could be called in question in any court of law except where the determination was questioned on the ground that it was contrary to natural justice, that is, that the FCC had adopted a *procedure* that was unfair. All this represented a compromise between those who wanted full access to the courts from decisions of the FCC and those who wanted to exclude the courts from the kind of supervision the Lords adopted in the case.

This question of the proper limits of supervision by the courts of decisions made by tribunals like the FCC which are designed to be independent of all other bodies, with the power, as the Minister said, to 'actually take the decision and actually distribute the money', is always controversial. The courts fight very hard against any statutory provisions which exclude them. *Padfield* and *Anisminic* represent considerable extensions of the power of the courts to intervene.

Later, in *Re Racal Communications Ltd*[22] Lord Diplock said:

> The break-through made by *Anisminic* was that, as respects administrative tribunals and authorities, the old distinction between errors of law that went to jurisdiction and errors of law that did not, was for practical purposes abolished. Any error of law that could be shown to have been made by them in the course of reaching their decision on matters of fact or of administrative policy would result in their having asked themselves the wrong question with the result that the decision they reached would be a nullity.

Industrial relations

After the war ended in 1945, there was (as in 1918) a natural optimism but an awareness of the dangers of a boom and slump like that of 1919–20.[23] In May 1944 the coalition Government had published a White Paper which promised the maintenance of 'a high and stable level of employment after the war'. During the period of the first post-war Labour Government 1945–50, after demobilization was complete, unemployment fell to below 300,000 and never exceeded 400,000 except for a short period of emergency in February and March 1947 caused by a fuel shortage. Similarly there was no inflation comparable with that of 1919–20. Partly this was because the Labour Government was able to influence trade unions to keep wage levels down.

During the war Ernest Bevin, formerly general secretary of the Transport and General Workers' Union, was Minister of Labour and ensured that the unions took part in the machinery of government. This continued under the Attlee Government from 1945 but at the same time negotiation on wages and conditions of work became more localized, with a large role for shop stewards, and resulted in a growth of unofficial strikes with important later consequences, as we shall see. In the later 1940s, such strikes became more widespread and more serious, especially in the docks, leading to declarations of states of emergency and the use of troops for unloading ships.

The early 1950s were adversely affected by rearmament after the outbreak of the Korean War but the Conservative Government was committed to full employment and stable prices. This was very largely maintained during the decade, unemployment generally being kept to 1 per cent or 2 per cent. Production expanded in the period 1953–5 but a wage-driven inflation began to develop and the Conservative Government was less successful than Labour had been in stabilizing prices and wages.

In 1957 increasing wage costs were worrying the Chancellor of the Exchequer (Thorneycroft), inflation was rising and the bank rate was increased from 5 per cent to 7 per cent. He received little support for his proposals on how to deal with the crisis and resigned on 6 January 1958. Relaxation of monetary constraints and other reliefs helped the Conservatives to a third election success in 1959. But relations with the trade union movement deteriorated, some writers attributing this in part to the election of Frank Cousins as general secretary of the Transport and General Workers' Union.[24]

The Conservatives during the 1950s were not in the business of 'taking on' the unions and managed pragmatically, by appointing committees of inquiry and giving way when faced with strong opposition, to keep industrial peace. Nor were the employers otherwise inclined. To some it seemed that the new corporatism was the solution to the conflicts in capitalism. In 1960, Seymour Martin Lipset could write:

> The fundamental political problems of the industrial revolution have been solved: the workers have achieved industrial and political citizenship; the conservatives have accepted the welfare state; and the democratic left has recognized that an increase in overall state power carries with it more dangers to freedom than solutions to economic problems.[25]

The economic situation worsened in 1960 and the bank rate was raised again for a short period. Wages continued to rise sharply. On 25 July 1961 restrictive measures were taken and the Chancellor of the Exchequer (Selwyn Lloyd) called for a pay pause.

Cairncross calls this 'an entirely new chapter in incomes policy'[26] as attempts were made by the Government to regulate wages in the private sector and to impose restraint in the public sector. In 1962, with a new Chancellor (Maudling), the National Incomes Commission was created to review wage proposals but with no powers of compulsion. The unions, who had not been consulted and had no representatives on the Commission, opposed its activities. Incomes policy was not showing signs of success. But unemployment remained low and, for those in work, living standards continued to rise.

During the early 1960s, relations between the Government and the unions were becoming more strained as the Chancellor, faced with another balance of payments crisis, sought to limit wages. Unofficial strikes became even more common. Kenneth Morgan writes of this time as of 'a society that was losing some of its wartime apparent cohesion and sense of shared values'.[27] The great majority of strikes were unofficial, without union backing, and disputes were locally negotiated between shop stewards and managers in the private sector, especially in the major manufacturing, engineering and construction industries and in the coal fields. In the late 1950s and early 1960s there was an 'explosion of militancy that accompanied the consolidation of shop steward power in the car industry'. In 1953–5 the average annual number of days lost in car firms was 137,000; in 1962–4, it was 321,000.[28]

These many pressures resulted in an attempt to bring both sides of industry into formal relationship with the Government when in 1962 the National Economic Development Council was set up and some measure of national planning was considered with the Trade Union Congress (somewhat reluctantly) becoming involved in the enterprise.

During this period from 1945 to the early 1960s, recourse to the courts was almost unknown as a means of resolving industrial disputes or challenging industrial practices. There had indeed been very little legislation affecting trade union activity since the beginning of the century although in both world wars strikes and lock-outs were made illegal and after 1945 the ban was continued for six years though not invoked.

Collective bargaining between the two sides of industry in the

United Kingdom has traditionally been conducted on a 'voluntary' or autonomous basis, not directly regulated by legal rules and not involving the courts as arbiters or decision-makers. Towards the end of the nineteenth century, the judges were reluctant to abandon their common-law view of combinations of workmen as conspiracies but legislation progressively relieved trade union activities of the taint first of criminality and then of tortious (civil) wrongdoing. When strikes and lock-outs occurred they were eventually settled – won, or lost, or compromised – by the parties to the dispute. The most significant statute was the Trade Disputes Act of 1906 which provided in section 1:

> An act done in pursuance of an agreement or combination by two or more persons shall, if done in contemplation or furtherance of a trade dispute, not be actionable unless the act, if done without any such agreement or combination would be actionable.

Section 3 provided:

> An act done by a person in contemplation or furtherance of a trade dispute shall not be actionable on the ground only that it induces some other person to break a contract of employment or that it is an interference with the trade, business or employment of some other person to dispose of his capital or his labour as he wills.

These two sections meant that workmen could not be proceeded against in the courts either because they had come together to pursue a common cause; or because they had persuaded others to join them in strike or other industrial action. But in both cases this protection extended only to those contemplating or furthering a trade dispute.

Although, in law, each trade unionist had a separate contract of employment with his employer, negotiations over terms and conditions, including wage rates, were usually conducted by trade union officials at national level. This was the meaning of collective bargaining.

In 1958 the Conservative Inns of Court Association published the pamphlet *A Giant's Strength*. It saw the problem of industrial action as 'how to retain the right to strike while limiting its scope to the minimum necessary to give the worker sufficient countervailing power against his employer' and proposed the creation of an independent tribunal, and the registration of trade unions with model rules, protection under the legislation of 1906 and other privileges being available only to such unions. The authors believed such measures would reduce the incidence of unofficial strikes which were seen by many as an unacceptable exercise of power.[29]

Suddenly, in the early 1960s 'the courts evidently became minded to reconsider the position of trade unions before law. Notably in *Rookes* v. *Barnard* in 1964 the Lords brought trade unions back into the toils of tort.'[30]

Rookes was a skilled draughtsman employed by British Overseas Airways Corporation and worked in a closed shop (where every employee was required, by agreement between the employers and the union, to be a union member). He left the union after an argument. Two shop stewards and a full-time union official threatened to call a strike if Rookes was not dismissed. BOAC lawfully terminated his contract and Rookes sued the three union officials for damages.[31]

The first question was whether the defendants had acted unlawfully at all. They had not offered violence or threats of violence (which would have amounted to the crime of intimidation). Could it be said that the threat to induce others to break their contracts by striking was nevertheless wrongful? At the trial the judge thought so and the jury awarded £7,500 damages. The Court of Appeal (Sellers, Donovan and Pearson L JJ) thought not and held that, in any event, the defendants were protected from liability by the Trade Disputes Act 1906 (above). But the Law Lords (Reid, Evershed, Hodson, Devlin and Pearce) took the opposite view and reversed the Court of Appeal.

The right to strike, which may include action falling short of full-scale withdrawal of labour, although not protected expressly by law, is as fundamental as the right to free speech. A person may enter into a contract with an employer under which he promises to work in exchange for payment. But, in a society which calls itself free, that person must not be prevented from withdrawing his labour, or taking other similar action. It may be that in so doing he breaks his contract and for this his employer may legally respond by dismissing him. But if criminal sanctions, such as fining or imprisonment, could be imposed for the breach then the contract of employment becomes oppressive. No man should be forced to work or to continue to work for another.

This is the way in which trade unionists saw the decision of the Law Lords: as an invasion of the right to strike. It seemed to reverse the intention behind the Trade Disputes Act of 1906 which sought to legalize certain action, in limited circumstances, in order to protect this fundamental right. Lord Reid said:

> Threatening a breach of contract may be a much more coercive weapon than threatening a tort, particularly when the threat is directed against a company or corporation, and, if there is no technical reason requiring a distinction between different kinds of threats, I can see no other ground for making any such distinction. . . . Intimidation of any kind appears to me to be highly objectionable. The law was not slow to prevent it when violence and threats of violence were the most effective means. Now the subtle means are at least equally effective I see no reason why the law should have to turn a blind eye on them. We have to tolerate intimidation by means which have been held to be lawful but these I would stop.

Lord Devlin said that he found 'nothing to differentiate a threat of a breach of contract from a threat of physical violence' and although he recognized the argument that 'the strike weapon' was now 'so generally sanctioned that it cannot really be regarded as an unlawful weapon of intimidation' he concluded that this could only be accepted if the courts were prepared 'either to hobble the common law in all classes of disputes lest its range is too wide to suit industrial disputes or to give the statute a wider scope than it was ever intended to have'.

In *Rookes* v. *Barnard* the Law Lords changed the law as radically in the complex field of industrial relations as any statute. The decision is to be placed alongside those other major innovatory decisions of the 1960s which I have already discussed earlier in this chapter. Once again Lord Reid, as senior Law Lord, gave the leading opinion, though Lord Devlin gave the most comprehensive judgment and two of their Lordships (Hodson and Pearce) limited themselves to footnotes.

It appears that, after hearing the initial arguments, a majority of their Lordships (perhaps all, except Lord Devlin) were in favour of dismissing the appeal, but that eventually there was a unanimous decision to allow it.[32] Wedderburn observes: 'What stands out in the speeches of the Law Lords is their determination to reach this result.'[33]

Six months after the decision in *Rookes* v. *Barnard*, the Law Lords (Reid, Radcliffe, Pearce, Upjohn and Donovan) reversed the Court of Appeal again, further limiting the application of the Trade Disputes Act 1906. Two trade unions – one organizing most of the watermen in the Port of London, the other being the Transport and General Workers' Union – sought to negotiate a general recognition agreement with a subsidiary company of Stratford & Sons who hired out barges in the Port. All but three workmen in the company belonged to the watermen's union, but agreement was made between the company and the T&GWU without consulting or informing the watermen's union. As a result, that union blacked barges hired out by Stratford's. The Court of Appeal (Lord Denning MR, Salmon and Pearson L JJ) held that this gave rise to a trade dispute within the meaning of the Act of 1906, which protected the watermen's union from suit. But the Law Lords held that it was only an inter-union dispute and so did not fall within that definition; and that the watermen's union had committed the tort of inducing breaches of the hiring contracts and of their members' contracts of employment.[34]

The immediate problem for the Labour Government when it took office in October 1964 was a crisis in the balance of payments and throughout the next six years the main domestic preoccupation of the Government was to seek to control increases in wages and prices, to prevent strikes, to restrain inflation, and to protect the pound sterling.

The Wilson administration began by making a compact with trade union leaders under which wage demands were to be restrained along with price increases. A national Board for Prices and Incomes was set up, soon made statutory. Standstills, pauses and restraints were sought to be imposed under Prices and In-comes Acts. These measures had some success but there were several serious stoppages, notably the seamen's strike for six-and-a-half weeks in 1966, an unofficial dock strike at Liverpool in 1967, and railway strikes in 1967 and 1968. In the event, sterling was devalued in November 1967.

In their effect on the economy the growth of unofficial strikes (without union approval) and unconstitutional strikes (in breach of agreed procedures) was a serious problem for the Government.[35] So also was the interpretation of the law as reflected by the decisions in *Rookes* v. *Barnard* and *Stratford*. In 1965 a Royal Commission was appointed with wide terms of reference: 'to consider relations between managements and employees and the role of trade unions and employers' associations in promoting the interests of their members and in accelerating the social and economic advance of the nation, with particular reference to the Law affecting the activities of these bodies'.

The Royal Commission was chaired by Lord Donovan, a former Labour MP who had been appointed a Lord of Appeal in 1964. The Commission reported in June 1968.[36] It began by contrasting the two systems of industrial relations which, it said, operated in Britain. One was 'the formal system embodied in the official in-stitutions'. The other was 'the informal system created by the actual behaviour of trade unions and employers' associations, of managers, shop stewards and workers'. The defect of this second system was that it was ill-regulated. The Commission referred to the strain created 'by the transfer of authority in industrial rela-tions to the factory and the workshop'. Workplace bargaining was 'largely autonomous', and fragmented.[37]

The Commission made many proposals for the strengthening of collective bargaining. But 'in present circumstances, no pro-posal to impose legal sanctions on individuals in breach of procedure agreements is practicable if it relies on enforcement by the em-ployer.' Experience had shown that criminal proceedings would not be successful. But if the reforms recommended by the Com-mission were implemented then it would be possible 'to identify any circumstances in which it would be neither unjust nor futile to apply legal sanctions.'[38]

Essentially therefore the Commission recommended the continuance of the voluntary system for the settlement of industrial disputes, and sought to introduce more formality, regularity and order into the negotiations on the shopfloor.

But the Prime Minister noted that 'on the specific question of unconstitutional strikes, the Commission recorded frankly that they had sought hard to find an interim remedy but had failed' although 'the use of the law, as a sanction or a deterrent, they specifically ruled out'.[39]

As this point in the developing story, the Court of Appeal (Lord Denning MR, Russell and Winn L JJ) made a further contribution. Local officials of the Transport and General Workers' Union called a strike of workers at the Torbay Hotel, Torquay, when the hotel refused to recognize the union. The manager of the nearby Imperial Hotel, in a speech, said the Hoteliers' Association would 'stamp out' the T&GWU. The Imperial had no T&GWU members but the hotel was picketed and a dispute declared. Esso supplied oil under contract to the Imperial and one of the local union officials said the union would cut off supplies to the hotel. The Imperial was granted injunctions against the union officials for procuring breach of contracts for the supply of oil and for picketing. The Court of Appeal on 17 December 1968 held that the action against the Imperial Hotel was not in furtherance of a trade dispute (and so protected by the Trade Disputes Act 1906), because the only dispute within the meaning of the Act was that between the union and the Torbay Hotel.[40] In this, and in other ways, this decision limited the meaning of a protected 'trade dispute'.

Barbara Castle was Secretary of State for Employment and Productivity and, on receiving the report of the Royal Commission, she began formal discussions with both sides of industry. Some six months later, on 17 January 1969, she published her policy paper *In Place of Strife*.[41]

The paper stated: 'Britain's special problem in industrial relations arises not from official strikes and lock-outs but from sudden industrial action taken before adequate negotiation or discussion of the problems has taken place.' Moreover, 95 per cent of all strikes were unofficial and were responsible for 75 per cent of all lost working days. The paper proposed that the Secretary of State should be given reserve discretionary powers to order a 'conciliation' pause requiring a return to work for twenty-eight days; and to enable the Secretary of State to order a ballot of trade union members involved on whether or not industrial action should be taken. A new Industrial Board would be able to impose fines recoverable in the county court by attachment of earnings and other civil remedies for the collection of debts but 'there will be no liability to imprisonment in default of payment or on account of failure to obey an Order'.[42]

Trade union leaders opposed these 'penal' clauses, partly because the possibility of being fined for striking suggested the introduction of a 'taint of criminality'; partly because the provisions seemed one-sided in that owners or managers of companies were scarcely subjected to any such proceedings whereas their decisions might be pre-emptive of union activity; and partly because any conciliation 'pause' might mean that trade unionists would be required to work on terms and conditions 'not acceptable to them but externally dictated'.[43] There was also opposition from some Labour back-bench MPs, and from others within the party, including James Callaghan (then Home Secretary) and other Ministers.

Discussions continued, as did unofficial strikes, but in mid April the Government announced its intention to introduce an interim Industrial Relations Bill including the penal clauses.

The many and diverse views within the trade union and Labour movement on the issues raised by the policy statement were strongly held. They reflected the feelings on the fundamental right to strike, on the position of trade unions as a necessary part of a pluralist society, on the perceived limits of the role of government. During the seamen's strike in 1966, Harold Wilson had accused the union of being dominated by 'a tightly knit group of politically motivated' men, naming eight members of the Communist party on the union's executive committee. Suspicions of such subversion within the trade union movement pushed the 'right' and the 'left' groups further apart. But, perhaps above all, there was widespread antagonism to the involvement of legal procedures, of the use of 'the law' to enforce changes in practice and procedures. The judges had long been seen as an enemy because of their attempted restrictions on trade union activity in the late nineteenth and early twentieth century. And it was recognized then, what came to be a reality soon thereafter, that imprisonment was the ultimate method of enforcement.

According to Harold Wilson's account the Government told the Trades Union Congress that if they would come forward with their own measures to deal with unofficial strikes, these would be considered as an alternative to the proposed legislation.[44] On the other hand the impression was also being given from inside the Government that the Bill must be supported by Labour backbenchers under a threat of dissolution of Parliament. Wilson's leadership was itself being challenged at this time by some Labour MPs. On 9 May at a joint meeting of the Cabinet and the national executive committee of the Labour party, James Callaghan 'intervened with a speech which was taken by a number of ministers as dissociating from Cabinet policies, particularly on the Industrial Relations Bill' to quote Wilson again.[45] This was leaked to the press and Callaghan ceased to be a member of the inner Cabinet which Wilson had created as a management committee.

The Government was now in some disarray, with strikes and demonstrations against the Bill, but also with many meetings with trade union leaders, in May and early June. Opposition from the TUC to the penal clauses continued with no sign of let up, the union leaders being again pressed by the Government to produce alternative union-directed procedures to control unofficial strikes. The dispute finally ended on 18 June with a solemn and binding undertaking (subsequently known as Solomon Binding) that the TUC, where it considered the workers were at fault, would place 'an obligation on trade unions to take energetic action within their rules' to end unofficial strikes. The Government withdrew its Bill. So, for a time, legal sanctions as a remedy for unofficial or unconstitutional industrial action were not enacted.

The strikes continued. But the national economy in general and the balance of payments in particular began to look more healthy early in 1970 when Wilson called an election which everyone (except, it is said, Mr Heath) expected Labour to win but which resulted in a respectable Conservative majority of thirty seats overall.

Retrospect

As already indicated, Lord Reid exerted a great influence over the development of public law during the 1960s. Every judge has to develop his own view of the judicial function and of the way that function relates to the Parliament and Executive. In this sense, every judge has to develop his own political philosophy. He must also develop his own jurisprudence, that is to say his view of the nature of law itself, what he sees as its bases and its purposes.

Reid was not a literalist like Simonds when interpreting statute law, as *Padfield* and *Anisminic* show. Indeed his search for the purpose or intention of legislation in both these cases took him some distance from the words of the statutory provisions. Not surprisingly, his development of the common law in *Burmah Oil*, *Ridge* and *Conway* was even freer.

Reid was never prepared to go so far as Denning[46] in attempts to depart from earlier common-law precedents or to impose his own interpretation of statutory provisions. And his approach was much more principled and consistent. Writing about common-law judgments, Reid remarked that judges had sometimes allowed doctrine to develop in a way that could easily cause injustice. Then, he said, 'In so far as we appellate judges can get the thing back on the rails let us do so.' But 'if it has gone too far we must pin our hopes on Parliament'.[47]

Reid had a conventional view about the virtues of judge-made law over statute. He said:

If you think in months, want an instant solution for your problems and don't mind that it won't wear well, then go for legislation. If you think in decades, prefer orderly growth and believe in the old proverb more haste less speed, then stick to the common law.[48]

Such language partakes of a more leisured age when social problems admitted of long examination. Waiting for the judges to arrive at mature solutions to the problems of the late twentieth century might prove a little too relaxed.

Reid also had a very English (rather than Scottish) attitude to general propositions. 'We are here', he said, 'to serve the public, the common ordinary reasonable man. He has no great faith in theories and he is quite right.'[49] The national motto of the English, he said, and we must assume he was speaking as a Scot, ought to be 'an ounce of fact is worth a ton of theory', a sentiment with which he did not quarrel.[50]

Pragmatism and the reasonable man were his often repeated themes:

> If the law is to keep in step with movements of public opinion then the judges must know how ordinary people of all grades of society think and live. You cannot get that from books or courses of study. You must have mixed with all kinds of people and get to know them. If you only listen to those who have hit the headlines you get quite the wrong impression. If we are to remain a democratic people those who try to be guided by public opinion must go to the grass roots. That is why it is so valuable for a judge to have given public service of some kind in his earlier days.[51]

And again:

> Our business as lawyers today is still to keep in mind the man of reason by preserving and developing a coherent body of legal principle, while at the same time going as far as we can to satisfy the modern pragmatic reasonable man. . . . The law departs at its peril from the views of the reasonable man.[52]

As we have seen, Reid served for many years as a constituency MP in urban Scotland in his forties and fifties, preceded by active service in the First World War. He brought to his long years as a Law Lord far wider experience outside the legal profession than most of his judicial brethren. In 1972 he urged 'the powers that be' to see to it that the new race of judges were 'men of the world'. If they were they could be trusted 'to acquaint themselves with public policy and apply it in a reasonable way to such new problems as will arise from time to time'.[53]

Nevertheless his formulations beg many questions. Lord Reid's view of what was 'reasonable' and of when previous decisions had or had not 'gone too far' must inevitably be controversial. For example, my subjective judgment applauds Reid's decision in *Conway* v. *Rimmer* but finds that in *Padfield* to be perverse and that in the case of the thalidomide children[54] to be mistaken. That is the statement of a political preference and judges make their own as do academic commentators who may also have some practical political experience. Reid decided public law cases out of a set of his own legal and political attitudes which were substantial. But, inevitably, they were his own.

He drew his own line between the role of Parliament and the role of the judiciary and if he felt the courts could not, on the state of the existing law, come to a just decision, had no reluctance in calling for legislative reform. Where possible, he promoted what he saw as the merits of the case before him over what he saw as the technicalities.

Reid was, perhaps, the best example of the advantages and disadvantages of a judge having had intimate knowledge of public administration and of politics. In *Conway* v. *Rimmer* he was willing to exert the authority of the judiciary over the prerogative claims of Ministers but his patrician attitude to the 'ill-informed' and 'captious' critics of Government 'without adequate knowledge' and with 'some axe to grind' partakes more of the Scottish grandee than of the political sceptic. Like most of those who have been part of the machinery of government, he was torn between his wish to protect those in power ('the business of government is difficult enough as it is')[55] and his willingness to hold them to account in general terms.

Lord Morris Borth-y-Gest was an important player in this dramatic change in judicial attitudes in the 1960s. He stood second in seniority to Reid whom he supported in *Ridge*, *Conway* and, later, in the case of the thalidomide children.[56] Socially his background was not typical of most of his brethren. His father was a bank manager, his earlier education at the Liverpool Institute, thence to Trinity Hall Cambridge. But, most unusually, he spent time at Harvard Law School. After a distinguished war career, he was an unsuccessful Liberal candidate for membership of the House of Commons in 1923 and 1924. In 1945 he became a judge in the King's Bench Division, a Lord Justice in the Court of Appeal from 1951 to 1960, and a Law Lord from 1960 to 1975. All speak of his courtesy, kindness and devotion to duty and there has been a tendency to treat him with a degree of condescension. But his attitude in the central dispute of the 1960s about the role of the judiciary in its relationship to the power of public authorities is more sophisticated than that of Lord Reid. His dissents in *Padfield* and *Anisminic* reflected a recognition of the deep problem which lay behind the conflicts between the judiciary and the executive. He was closer to Lord Greene in his attempt to arrive at a conclusion which was, in terms of political philosophy, thought through. Neither the superficiality of Denning nor the pragmatism of Reid was good enough for him.

In these seven decisions – *Ridge, Burmah Oil, Padfield, Conway, Anisminic; Rookes, Stratford* – the House of Lords, led by Lord Reid, restored the position of the highest court to a position of some eminence.

In *Ridge* the way was opened for a much wider review of the propriety of the exercise of administrative action, untrammelled by preconceptions or categories. The decision in *Burmah Oil* showed a willingness to invent legal rights which had not previously existed, and, like *Conway*, was a direct rebuttal of Ministerial claims. *Padfield* and *Anisminic* went much further, biting into the red meat of statutory powers. *Rookes* and *Stratford* made a strong impact on the politics of the day, reinforcing the belief of trade unionists that the courts were biased against them. The question that remains unanswered is why, at this particular time, the Law Lords (led by Devlin who was crucially supported by Reid) became 'minded' to reopen the liability of trade unions. *Rookes* v. *Barnard* was decided at first instance (by Sachs J) as early as May 1961, by the Court of Appeal in April 1962, and not until January 1964 by the Law Lords. During these three years the image of consensual sweetness and light so wrongly portrayed by Lipset[57] was being rudely shattered by the growth of industrial strife. Perhaps the Law Lords were quick to reflect this change in atmosphere.

In these two main areas of Ministerial powers and industrial relations, the Law Lords in the 1960s became positive and active.

Ridge v. *Baldwin* (March 1963) and *Rookes* v. *Barnard* (January 1964) pointed the way and judicial attitudes were formed which were to be developed over the next twenty-five years.

Notes

1   Proceedings of standing committee on National Health Service Bill on 26 June 1946 col 1762, 1770; and 425 HC Deb. col 1978–2004 (23 July 1946).
2   Devlin's early retirement in 1964 deprived the Law Lords of an outstanding judge.
3   See note 15 below.
4   Alan Paterson, 'Scottish Lords of Appeal', in *The Juridical Review* (1988), p. 251, note 57.
5   *Ridge* v. *Baldwin* [1963] 1 QB 539.
6   [1964] AC 40. In the majority were Lords Reid, Morris, Hodson and Devlin; Lord Evershed dissented.
7   See above, pp. 41–4.
8   *R.* v. *Electricity Commissioners ex parte London Electricity Joint Committee Co.* [1924] 1 KB 171.
9   Lord Hewart CJ in *R.* v. *Legislative Committee of the Church Assembly ex parte Haynes-Smith* [1928] 1 KB 411.
10 See above, pp. 58–9.
11 *Burmah Oil Co.* v. *Lord Advocate* [1965] AC 75.
12 For a full account see Blom-Cooper and Drewry, *Final Appeal* (1972), pp. 368–73.
13 *Conway* v. *Rimmer* [1968] AC 910.
14 *Duncan* v. *Cammell, Laird & Co.* [1942] AC 624.
15 In 1966 the Law Lords abandoned their rule that they were bound by their earlier decisions: [1966] 1 WLR 1234.
16 [1968] AC 997.
17 781 HC Deb. col *46–7* (31 March 1969).
18 475 HC Deb. col 41 (8 May 1950).
19 [1969] 2 AC 223 n.
20 [1968] 2 QB 862.
21 *Anisminic Ltd.* v. *Foreign Compensation Commission* [1969] 2 AC 147; Lords Morris Borth-y-Gest and Pearson dissented.
22 [1981] AC 374.
23 See above, p. 1.

24   Alec Cairncross, *The British Economy since 1945* (1992), p. 113.
25   S.M. Lipset, *Political Man* (1960), p. 406, quoted in David Coates, *The Crisis of Labour* (1989), p. 8.
26   See note 24, p. 114; Cairncross was at this time (1961) Economic Adviser to the Government.
27   Morgan, *The People's Peace* (1990), p. 238.
28   Coates, *The Crisis of Labour* (1989), p. 25.
29   H. Phelps Brown, *The Origins of Trade Union Power* (1983), Chapter X.
30   Ibid., p. 172.
31   *Rookes* v. *Barnard* [1964] AC 1129.
32   A. Paterson, *The Law Lords* (1982), p. 119.
33   K.W. Wedderburn, *The Worker and the Law* (3rd edn, 1986), p. 42. In 1965, under the Labour Government, another Trade Disputes Act was passed which, in part, reversed *Rookes* v. *Barnard*.
34   *Stratford* v. *Lindley* [1965] AC 269.
35   Law Lords were frequently used to preside over inquiries seeking settlement of disputes. Between May 1964 and August 1968 Lord Pearson was called in over strikes in electricity supply, airways and steel; and three times in ports and shipping industries.
36   Cmnd 3623. In April 1968 the Conservative party published 'A Fair Deal at Work', proposing a cooling-off period for strikes and compulsory registration of unions.
37   Cmnd 3623 (see note 36 above), paras 46, 61, 66, 67, 68.
38   Ibid., paras 1054, 1055.
39   Harold Wilson, *The Labour Government 1964–70* (1974 edn), p. 681.
40   *Torquay Hotel* v. *Cousins* [1969] 2 Ch. 106.
41   Cmnd 3888.
42   Cmnd 3888 (see note 41 above), paras 86, 88, 90, 93, 62.
43   See Phelps Brown, *Origins of Trade Union Power* (1983), p. 178.
44   Wilson, *The Labour Government 1964–70* (1974), p. 808; 781 HC Deb. col 990 (15 April 1969).
45   Wilson, *The Labour Government 1964–70* (1974), p. 816.
46   See above, p. 58.
47   'The Law and the Reasonable Man', in *Proceedings of the British Academy 1968*, p. 193.
48   'The Judge as Law Maker', in XII JSPTL (1972), p. 22.
49   Ibid.
50   See note 47 above.
51   See note 48 above.
52   See note 47 above.

53   See note 48 above.
54   *Att-Gen* v. *Times Newspapers* [1974] AC 273; see below, pp. 116–7.
55   See above, p. 86.
56   See below, p. 117.
57   See above, p. 93.

5 The divided seventies

The decade began with three years and nine months of Conservative rule under Edward Heath and continued with five years and two months of Labour rule under Harold Wilson and James Callaghan. As we shall see,[1] industrial relations, within the general economic context, was the battlefield for much of the political conflict. To this conflict, judicial decision-making, in its interpretation of the new, and re-interpretation of the old, legislation made its own considerable contribution.

In five other cases, concerning freedom of speech, Ministerial powers, and security, the courts developed further their own positive and activist jurisprudence. The first of these received wide publicity.

The thalidomide litigation

Judges are often thought of, in the words of Lord Atkin, as standing 'between the subject and any attempted encroachments on his liberty by the executive, alert to see that any coercive action is justified in law'.[2] But the demands of those holding political or economic power sometimes persuade judges to adopt other positions. Principles like freedom from arbitrary arrest and freedom of speech are met with arguments based on the claims of special interests to be treated exceptionally. Sometimes these claims are so broad, like that of national security, that they seem to cover the whole of the principle. An allegation of imprisonment without legal authority may be pursued by seeking the issue of a writ of habeas corpus requiring the person responsible for holding the individual in custody to justify his exercise of power. But although great lip service is paid to the principle, both inside and outside the courts, it is not unusual for some special reason to be found by the judge for not ordering the release.

Curtailment of freedom of speech is frequently said to be justified on the basis of the requirements of a fair trial, or of confidentiality, or of the protection of the reputation of others, or of public morality, or of the prevention of disorder or crime, or of national security. None of the so-called fundamental freedoms is absolute and all those grounds of exception may in particular circumstances be acceptable. Indeed the extent to which individual freedom exists in a society is largely determined by the interaction between those principles and these exceptions. Grand-sounding statements in constitutions or Bills of Rights may afford little protection if judges are willing to allow them to be easily subverted by the pleas of official or special interests. Judges exercise their powers of interpretation and of enforcement in accordance with their own views of the rival claims of the individual and those interests. Their views will no doubt be influenced by the whole ambience of society, by tradition, by the climate of opinion. But ultimately the decisions of where to draw the lines will be theirs.

To understand how remarkable was the decision of the Law Lords in the thalidomide case it is necessary to trace the story in some detail. Censorship, in the form of an injunction issued by a court of law to prevent the publication by a national newspaper of an article concerning a matter of the greatest public interest, is never easy to defend. For the countervailing special interest to be preferred calls for a most compelling justification. The decision of the Law Lords in *Attorney-General* v. *The Times Newspapers*[3] rests on the reasons given by their Lordships for their major invasion of press freedom.

In October 1957, a German pharmaceutical company (Chemie Grünenthal) began to market a drug – known in the United Kingdom as thalidomide – which went on sale under fifty-one different names in eleven European, seven African, seventeen Asia, and eleven north and south American countries (excluding the USA). It was advertised as a completely safe, non-toxic sedative with no side-effects, completely safe for pregnant women. The drug was withdrawn in Britain, Germany, and some other countries in November 1961 but it continued to be available after this date in Japan, Sweden, Argentina, Canada and Italy, for many months. The main adverse effect of the drug resulted from its being taken between the fifth and eighth weeks of pregnancy. The foetus when born suffered from the condition known as phocomelia ('seal-limb') in which the hands or feet or both start immediately from the shoulder or hip, like the flippers of a seal; but also from other major deformities, some more severe, some less so. Worldwide there may have been as many as 10,000 cases. In Britain, where the drug was marketed by Distillers Ltd, there were over 400 such babies who survived and probably twice as many who died on birth.

During 1958, the manufacturers Grünenthal began to receive complaints from German doctors that patients on the drug were suffering from giddiness, and disturbance of balance. As sales figures rose dramatically during 1959, additional side-effects began to be described as sickness, trembling, polyneuritis and peripheral neuritis with numbness and cold in feet and ankles. Responsibility was denied by the manufacturers who, faced with the possibility that the drug might be put on prescription and not remain available over the counter, vigorously resisted the imputation that the drug was to blame. In early 1961 similar reports of peripheral neuritis were being made in Britain.

Thalidomide was introduced into New South Wales early in 1961 and, in May, Dr McBride, who had a large practice in obstetrics in Sydney and who had used the drug as a sedative, began to notice that the Women's Hospital in Sydney was recording an exceptional number of birth malformations. After failing to find any other common cause, he became convinced that thalidomide was to blame and on 13 June reported his suspicions to the Hospital which at once withdrew the drug. Dr McBride then telephoned the Australian branch of Distillers, as the responsible manufacturers, and told them of the reasons for the drug's withdrawal and suggested its promotion be stopped while an investigation was made. He was told his suspicions would be passed on to London but was asked not to spread his disquiet. On 6 July

1961, Dr McBride told Distillers' local salesman who said he would report it to the company immediately and later testified that he did so. The salesman said he told the managing director who told the chairman of the company. But the managing director denied this and the company insisted that no word of Dr McBride's suspicions reached the head office in London until 21 November 1961. In the meantime, says *The Sunday Times* account, Distillers

> continued to sell the drug in Australia as vigorously as it always had, and it remained on sale in Britain, Germany and elsewhere. How many mothers around the world took thalidomide in the four months between McBride's first warning and the withdrawal is not known.[4]

Dr McBride had much difficulty in persuading others in Australia that his suspicions were justified even after two more typical cases occurred in Sydney in September. But evidence was now mounting in Germany of the causal connection between thalidomide and birth deformities. After much pressure by Professor Lenz of Hamburg University and against much opposition and publicity in the German press, the company withdrew the drug on 26 November 1961.

Not surprisingly, claims for compensation began to be made on behalf of the deformed children. In the United Kingdom, Distillers Ltd denied that their negligence had caused the disaster. Under UK law it was not sufficient for the complainants to establish the causal connection between the taking of the drug and the consequent deformities. They had to show that Distillers were at fault, that at some stage in the preparation of the drug they had failed to take reasonable care.

The standard of care required of those who market drugs in these circumstances is no doubt high, but proving that it was not met is difficult, and expensive. The first group of complainants combined to negotiate with Distillers, some seventy actions having been instituted before 1968. A settlement was reached by which Distillers agreed to pay each claimant 40 per cent of the estimated damages which he or she would recover if the case were successfully pursued in court. Eventually sixty-five of these cases were settled on those terms, Distillers paying about £1 million in all. But, as publicity spread, more claims were made and by February 1969, 248 more writs had been served and the total figure of unsettled claims eventually rose to some 400.

Further negotiations took place and Distillers proposed to settle again by setting up a trust fund of over £3 million. But this scheme broke down because a few claimants would not agree to it and Distillers insisted that the acceptance had to be inclusive of all outstanding claims. An attempt to override the refusal by those claimants was rejected by the Court of Appeal.[5]

During this period since 1961, the Ministry of Health had given the parents little support and, along with much of the press, had taken the view that Distillers had done all they could reasonably have been expected to do to ensure the drug was safe. Solicitors representing the parents, and counsel instructed by them, also brought pressure to bear to persuade the parents to accept the deals offered by Distillers in some cases.

Some ten years had now passed since the drug was withdrawn and, apart from the first settlement, little progress had been made. Then the claimants found a champion in the editor of *The Sunday Times* newspaper, Harold Evans. Through his team of investigative journalists, he collected a great deal of material and on 24 September 1972 published 'a long and powerful article' as Lord Reid was to call it. Two general propositions were put forward. The first was that it should not be necessary for the claimants in cases like this (where the causal connection was admitted) to prove negligence. The second was that the currently accepted method of assessing damages was inadequate. The article then urged Distillers to 'offer much, much more to every one of the thalidomide victims'.

Distillers immediately brought this article to the attention of the Attorney-General asking him to take proceedings against *The Sunday Times* for contempt of court. But he took no action. The editor then had a second article prepared for publication and he sent this, first, to the Attorney. The editor could have simply published the article without informing the Attorney but if he had done so and if subsequently the courts had held that the second article was in contempt the penalty (fining or imprisonment) would have been severe. The Attorney now took the view that he should intervene and so sought an injunction against the owners of *The Sunday Times* to restrain them from publishing the second article. The Divisional Court on 17 November 1972 granted the injunction. Lord Widgery, Lord Chief Justice, said that the defendant newspaper was deliberately seeking to influence the settlement by the parties of the pending proceedings by bringing pressure to bear on Distillers and that it was not the function of the court in these cases to balance the competing interest in free speech. The article complained of, he said, traced the history of the development, marketing and testing of the drug in considerable detail and its publication would prejudice the free choice of Distillers to conduct their litigation as they thought fit.[6]

The *Sunday Times* article of 24 September 1972 aroused Mr Jack Ashley, the Labour MP who was chairman of the House of Commons All Party Committee on the Disabled. The campaign for the thalidomide children began to receive support in the media and on 29 November the House of Commons debated their plight,[7] shortly after the hearing on the injunction before the Divisional Court. Support came from all sides of the House, though the Government front bench remained neutral while agreeing that £3 million would be set aside for improving services for the congenitally disabled and that consideration would be given for setting up a trust fund after the litigation was concluded. On 19 December the Prime Minister announced the setting up of a Royal Commission on civil liability and compensation for personal injury.

Pressure was also exercised by a group of shareholders of Distillers and by the Trades Union Congress seeking greater compensation. They were able to persuade some large institutional investors including insurance companies and local authorities to express their disquiet. There were threats of a boycott of Distillers' products and the value of Distillers' shares fell sharply.

In January 1973, Distillers responded and offered to make ten annual payments of £2 million to a charitable trust. Eventually and after much discussion between lawyers and actuaries on both sides a settlement was reached by the High Court in July 1973. With additional sums the total commitment by Distillers was more than £28 million.

Meanwhile the *Sunday Times* had appealed against the decision of the Divisional Court. The Court of Appeal in February 1973 allowed the appeal and discharged the injunction on the principal ground that the public interest in free speech prevailed over that of ensuring a fair trial because the proceedings in this case were dormant. Lord Denning MR said that the public interest in having the matter discussed outweighed the prejudice that might be occasioned to a party to the dispute. Moreover, as Scarman LJ also said, there had been a debate in Parliament, so why should the courts apply stricter rules to prevent discussion? 'No party', said Phillimore LJ 'intends litigation'.[8]

Distillers appealed successfully to the House of Lords, and the injunction was restored.[9] Lord Reid gave the leading opinion delivered on 25 July 1973. He began by emphasizing that the law of contempt of court must be founded entirely on public policy and was not there to protect the private rights of parties to a litigation or prosecution. Public policy generally required a balancing of conflicting interests. 'Freedom of speech should not be limited to any greater extent than is necessary; but it cannot be allowed where there would be real prejudice to the administration of justice.'

Newspaper comment (in advance of or during the court hearing) might prejudice the matters on which witnesses gave evidence and on which the judge and jury made their findings. Lord Reid revealed that the second article, the subject of the case before the courts, consisted in the main of detailed evidence and argument intended to show that Distillers did not exercise due care to see that thalidomide was safe before they put it on the market. 'If this material were released now', said Lord Reid, 'it appears to me to be almost inevitable that detailed answers would be published and there would be expressed various public prejudgments of this issue. That I would regard as very much against the public interest.' He considered that 'trial by newspaper' was intrinsically objectionable. There will be 'ill-informed, slapdash or prejudiced attempts to influence the public'. Lord Reid called in aid that opinion of the reasonable or ordinary man on which, as we have seen, he liked to rely.

> What I think is regarded as most objectionable is that a newspaper or television programme should seek to persuade the public, by discussing the issues and evidence in a case before the court, whether civil or criminal, that one side is right and the other wrong. If we were to ask the ordinary man or even a lawyer in his leisure moments why he has that feeling, I suspect that the first reply would be – well look at what happens in some other countries where that is permitted.

This was said on 18 July 1973. Perhaps the ordinary man would today, in the light of recent experience of miscarriages of justice, place more faith in newspaper or television programmes than did Lord Reid; and also be less xenophobic.

Dealing with the reasons which induced the Court of Appeal to discharge the injunction, especially that the actions had been dormant for several years, Lord Reid noted that 'active negotiations for a settlement were going on all the time'. He was clearly of the view that in this case the public interest in protecting the administration of justice from interference prevailed over the public interest in free speech. As matters stood at present, the injunction should be continued.

The other Law Lords agreed that Distillers' appeal should be allowed. Lord Morris Borth-y-Gest thought the projected article went too far because it conveyed the message that an examination of the issue as to negligence showed there was a considerable case to be presented against Distillers. Lord Diplock, with whom Lord Simon agreed, said the article held Distillers up to public obloquy in their reliance on the defence that they were not guilty of any negligence. Lord Cross followed Lord Reid. He argued most strongly for preserving the contempt of court rules, even if there was no risk that publication might influence any subsequent hearing before a court, saying that one could not deal with a particular publication in isolation.

> A publication prejudging an issue in pending litigation which is itself innocuous enough may provoke replies which are far from

innocuous but which, as they are replies, it would seem very unfair to restrain. So gradually the public would become habituated
to, look forward to, and resent the absence of preliminary discussions in the 'media' of any case which aroused widespread interest. An absolute rule – though it may seem to be unreasonable if
one looks only to the particular case – is necessary to prevent a
gradual slide towards trial by newspaper or television.

Under the European Convention on Human Rights it is possible for any person to petition the Commission claiming to be the
victim of a violation by any of the nation states who had agreed to
be bound by the rights protected by the Convention as had the
United Kingdom. Article 10 of the Convention protects freedom
of expression, subject to many conditions. In January 1974 *The
Times* claimed that the injunction contravened this Article and
eventually in 1979 the European Court of Human Rights by eleven
votes to nine upheld the newspaper. This meant that the United
Kingdom was obliged to change the rules of the common law on
contempt of court to bring UK law into conformity with the
finding of the European Court. Avowedly for this purpose, amongst
others, the Contempt of Court Act 1981 was passed. It is doubtful
how far this primary aim was achieved. The Act provided that
liability for unintentional contempt of court should be limited.
But it also provided that nothing in the Act restricted liability for
contempt in respect of conduct intended to impede or prejudice
the administration of justice. So newspapers and others may still
be made subject to injunctions preventing publication if the court
imputes to them such an intention. And in *Attorney-General* v.
English[10] (1982) Lord Diplock seemed to say that the Act would
not have enabled the *Sunday Times* to publish their second thalidomide article because in that case 'the whole purpose of it was
to put pressure on that company in the lawful conduct of their
defence'.

The defect in the decision of the Law Lords in the thalidomide
case was their evaluation of where the public interest lay. The
proceedings thought to be prejudiced by the *Sunday Times* article
were far too remote in time. Indeed it was most improbable that
those proceedings would ever have reached the courts. And to

consider that Distillers Ltd needed the protection of the courts to withstand the pressures of public opinion was to take an absurd view of the rival strengths of the parents on the one hand and of one of the strongest and wealthiest corporations on the other. While Lords Reid, Morris and Cross were prepared to accept that it was legitimate to seek to influence litigants by forceful comments, Lords Diplock and Simon took a stricter line and seemed to say that even the first article in the *Sunday Times* might have been in contempt and that the public interest in press freedom should not be allowed to override the possibility of prejudice.

As the European Court found, there was no 'pressing social need' to justify this gross interference with press freedom. But, as we shall see, it set the pattern for similar judicial rulings over the next decade and a half. The Law Lords were, as they saw it, protecting their own system of administration of justice and this may in part account for their extreme position. Lord Reid himself, as we saw in his reference in *Conway* v. *Rimmer* to 'ill-informed or captious public or political criticism' (the other side of his coin of 'the reasonable man') was no committed protector of civil rights. Nor does the record of the other four Law Lords separate them from his attitude.

The Crossman diaries

In 1975 the *Sunday Times* again came into conflict with the Attorney-General of the day.[11] R.H.S. Crossman had been a member of the Cabinet in a Labour Government from 1964 to 1970. During these years he kept a diary of events with a view to publication. Before his death in April 1974 he completed and handed to his publishers the first volume covering the period 1964–6.

Constitutional practice requires that former Ministers who wish to publish memoirs of their years in office should send a copy, before publication, to the Secretary of the Cabinet (a senior civil servant) seeking his agreement. The Secretary, who is responsible to the Prime Minister, was at this time Sir John Hunt and his first reaction on reading this first volume in May and June 1974 was that he could not see how it could be published within the 'closed period' for Cabinet records (usually thirty years).

Sir John explained his opinion by saying that the conventions restricting publication flowed from the two complementary principles of the collective responsibility of the Government as a whole and the personal responsibility of individual Ministers. Records of Cabinet proceedings, he said, were secret to ensure completely frank discussion within Cabinet and to preserve mutual trust which needed to exist between Ministers and between Ministers and their senior advisers. Ministers might publish their memoirs but only after they had been 'cleared' by the Cabinet Secretary and, where necessary, the Prime Minister. Sir John said that what he called 'parameters' excluded four areas from report or discussion: Cabinet discussions; advice by civil servants; discussion on senior appointments; and other confidential discussions on policy clearly intended to be private.

Apart from these arguments between the publishers of the first volume and the Cabinet Secretary, there was a separate conflict. the *Sunday Times* had had since 1966 a contract to publish Crossman's memoirs. The newspaper now proposed to publish serialized and edited extracts from his diaries. The literary executors of the Crossman estate forwarded these in November 1974 to the Cabinet Secretary. He refused to give them clearance. On 26 January 1975, with the agreement of the executors, the *Sunday Times* nevertheless published its first extract.

In the event no action was taken against the *Sunday Times*. The newspaper submitted its proposed extracts in advance of publication on each occasion to the Cabinet Secretary for comment. But the newspaper took its own decisions on what to include or exclude. Much of the early extracts was relatively innocuous and, by 16 March, some 85,000 words had been published. On that date the extract was, to quote Hugo Young, 'Crossman's wholly indiscreet account of the July 1966 crisis, including the Cabinet argument for and against devaluation, and the line-up on each side.'

Crossman's executors thought that the serialization had cleared the way for the diaries volume to be published. But on 9 June 1975 the Attorney-General served a writ and moved for an injunction to restrain publication of the diaries and of any further serialization. The full trial of the action began on 22 July 1975 before the Lord Chief Justice, Lord Widgery, sitting alone.

This case of *Attorney-General* v. *Jonathan Cape Ltd and Times Newspapers*[12] was unusual in that the Cabinet Secretary gave oral evidence and was cross-examined by counsel for Times Newspapers who referred to those general rules or 'parameters' laid down by the Cabinet Secretary. Part of the cross-examination ran as follows.

Q. Do you notice parameter 1 speaks about 'recording or revealing detailed discussion in Cabinet or Cabinet Committee'? You notice the word 'detailed'?

A. Yes.

Q. And do you notice that runs through the next two as well, it is the starting word of the next two, 'Detailed discussions. . . . Detailed discussions'? Is there, according to you, importance to be attached to the word 'detailed'?

A. Yes.

Q. What importance?

A. . . . . In looking at memoirs, what this parameter is directed to is the protection of collective responsibility. By 'detailed discussions' I mean the detailed revelation of other Ministers' positions, the argument, the compromises, the points surrendered between them.

Q. Is it intended to mean, therefore, that an undetailed discussion is permissible?

A. No. This is intended to mean that we do not mean that there can be no references to Cabinet or Cabinet Committee discussions in diaries.

Q. Where do you draw the line, and who draws the line?

A. I think it is very difficult to draw the line, and that is why, in the correspondence with the *Sunday Times*, you will see frequent references to 'grey areas', and why, subject to stopping short at a point where collective responsibility and confidentiality would be gravely damaged, one has to leave it to a large extent to the judgment of the author.

Q. Exactly. Don't you think you have to leave it exclusively in the end to the judgment of the author?

A. No.

Throughout the whole of the discussions between the Cabinet Secretary and the *Sunday Times*, the former was concerned to draw attention to the passages which, in his opinion, offended against the parameters he had laid down which he claimed were derived from past practice. But, inevitably, this opinion was based on his interpretation of that practice as he applied the parameters to the texts put before him by the newspaper and the publishers. Part of those texts he considered not only innocuous but justified by the principle that former Ministers were entitled to put their own versions of events on record. Others he regarded as clearly infringing those parameters. In between, were the 'grey areas'. All these were political judgments. The question for the courts was whether any of these judgments were challengeable in law; and if so, on what criteria.

The Lord Chief Justice said that the Attorney-General had to show that the publication would be a breach of confidence; that the public interest required that publication be restrained; and that there were no other facets of the public interest contradictory of and more compelling than that relied upon. Moreover the court, when asked to restrain such a publication, must closely examine the extent to which relief was necessary to ensure that restrictions were not imposed beyond the strict requirement of public need. He decided that in this case the Attorney-General had made out his claim

> that the expression of individual opinions by Cabinet Ministers in the course of Cabinet discussions are matters of confidence, the publication of which can be restrained by the court when this is clearly necessary in the public interest.

Lord Widgery found also that the maintenance of the doctrine of joint responsibility within the Cabinet was in the public interest and that the application of that doctrine might be prejudiced by premature disclosure of the views of individual Ministers.

But the Lord Chief Justice came to the considered view that the publication at this interval of more than ten years after the recorded events would not inhibit free discussion in the Cabinet, even though the individuals were the same and the national problems had what he called a distressing similarity with those of a decade before. So he refused the injunction but accepted that there might be other applications later in regard to material other than that in volume 1.

The effect of this decision was ambivalent. On the one hand, publication was enabled to go ahead and resulted in the full publication of the three volumes of the diaries totalling (with editorial notes) some $1\frac{1}{2}$ million words. On the other hand, the decision established the principle that the courts were empowered to exercise control within the limits defined by the judge.

In April 1975 a Committee of Privy Councillors on Ministerial Memoirs was set up under the chairmanship of Lord Radcliffe. Its report was published in January 1976[13] and the Prime Minister stated that it was accepted by the Government.[14] The report largely restated the conventions applied by Sir John Hunt. Restrictions fell into three separate categories of information: national security; disclosures injurious to relations with other countries; information destructive of confidential relationships, in particular the opinions and attitudes of colleagues, the advice given by civil servants, his assessments of those who served under him. The proposed rules laid down by the Committee were not made enforceable by law and remained a voluntary code of conduct. On 1 July 1991, it was reported that in the past two years ten authors had submitted manuscripts to the head of the home civil service under these guidelines. They included four former Ministers whose books had subsequently been published. The Minister of State in the Privy Council Office said that 'by and large' the voluntary system worked 'reasonably well'.[15]

The Hosenball affair

The third case concerned the conflict between free speech and the claims of national security.

Mark Hosenball was an American student, educated at a Quaker school in England and at Trinity College Dublin. From 1973 to 1976 he worked at different times as a journalist in the United Kingdom having been granted permission to do so. Towards the end of 1976 the Home Secretary 'took offence at certain activities' of Mr Hosenball but as the Lord Chief Justice said 'we do not know precisely what they were'. Lord Denning said Hosenball had tried 'to obtain information of a very sensitive character'.

Mark Hosenball was associated with Philip Agee, also an American, who was a former agent of the Central Intelligence Agency of the USA and had written about the operations of that Agency. Both were served by the Home Secretary with deportation notices. Hosenball's notice said he had 'sought to obtain and obtained for publication information harmful to the security of the United Kingdom, and that this information included information prejudicial to the safety of the servants of the Crown'. For most of his journalistic career in the UK Hosenball was a staff writer for *Time Out*, a weekly magazine which was primarily an entertainment guide but also contained articles of a radical, investigatory and anti-establishment nature. Hosenball wrote about CIA agents in Britain and about Signals Intelligence which under the umbrella of the Government Communications Headquarters[16] operated a system around the world of listening to radio and electronic transmissions. In May 1976 *Time Out* published an article entitled 'The Eavesdroppers', under the authorship of Hosenball and Duncan Campbell, about the operations of Signals Intelligence. Some or all of these publications may have been the reason for the deportation order.[17]

Under the Immigration Act 1971, there is no right of appeal against such a deportation order but the Government set up a procedure under which a person served with such an order could make representations to a panel of three persons nominated by the Home Secretary. The representations could be made orally, not by a legal representative, although a friend could give assistance. Third parties could be called to testify on behalf of the deportee. No details of the grounds on which the order was made were given to the deportee, and evidence provided by the security service (or other persons) to the panel was not disclosed. The panel made a recommendation to the Home Secretary who was not bound to accept it. Agee and Hosenball each separately made their representations to the panel who consisted of a former British intelligence officer, a former Home Office civil servant and a trade union official. The orders were confirmed.[18]

In February 1977 Mark Hosenball applied to the High Court for the quashing of the order on the grounds that it was wrong in law, in breach of the rules of natural justice, and that the Home Secretary had misdirected himself. The essence of the argument was that Hosenball was entitled to a fair hearing which he had not received, particularly because he had not been supplied with sufficient information about the activities of which he was accused to enable him to defend himself.

The case was first heard by the Lord Chief Justice and two High Court judges who dismissed the application. On 29 March 1977 the appeal was heard by Lord Denning MR, Geoffrey Lane and Cumming-Bruce L JJ and rejected.[19] Lord Denning, in a now famous passage, said:

> There is a conflict between the interests of national security on the one hand and the freedom of the individual on the other. The balance between these two is not for a court of law. It is for the Home Secretary. He is the person entrusted by Parliament with the task. In some parts of the world national security has on occasion been used as an excuse for all sorts of infringements of individual liberty. But not in England. Both during the wars and after them successive ministers have discharged their duties to the complete satisfaction of the people at large. They have set up advisory committees to help them, usually with a chairman who has done everything he can to ensure that justice is done. They have never interfered with the liberty or the freedom of movement of any individual except where it is absolutely necessary for the safety of the state.

The orders were enforced and both men were deported in May 1977. A subsequent application to the European Commission of Human Rights was declared inadmissible.

Not for the first nor for the last time, Lord Denning sprang to the support of the needs of 'national security', though his abdication of all judicial responsibility in this case was extreme. Denning referred to the majority decision in *Liversidge* v. *Anderson*[20] with approval. His claim that hearings by the panel had given 'complete satisfaction' to all was unsupported and unsupportable. Denning's obeisance to 'national security' has in recent years been judicially followed in many cases where the circumstances were, as here, far removed from the sound of the clash of arms. Once principle is subordinated to expediency, the consequences are not easily controlled.

Tameside

Here we are back in *Padfield* country. In the 1970s, the reorganization of secondary education from selective school to comprehensive was still under way. The Labour-controlled borough of Tameside (which was the Local Education Authority) in March 1975 put forward proposals to this end to the Labour Secretary of State to come into effect in September 1976. In November 1975, they were approved. In May 1976 at the local elections the Conservatives won control of the borough council and so of the LEA and on 7 June told the Secretary of State that they proposed not to implement the approved plans. On 11 June the Secretary of State gave the council a direction requiring them to implement those plans and on 18 June the Divisional Court ordered the council to comply. On 26 July the Court of Appeal overruled the Divisional Court and on 2 August the appeal by the Secretary of State to the House of Lords was dismissed.[21]

The statutory authority empowering the Secretary of State to give directions was contained in section 68 of the Education Act 1944, which provided that if he was satisfied that a Local Education Authority had acted or was proposing to act unreasonably he might give such direction as appeared to him to be expedient.

The ground on which the Secretary of State based the exercise of this discretionary power was that the Conservatives' change of plan would give rise to considerable difficulties because they would have insufficient time between June and September 1976 to set up a proper selection process. The LEA argued that they would be able to do so and the Court of Appeal heard fresh evidence to support this contention.

There were two questions. The first concerned the practicability of the Conservative proposal. Here the Minister and the LEA disagreed. The second concerned the legal limits to be placed on the apparently wide discretionary power of the Minister to give a direction. The Court of Appeal held that it was not enough for the Minister to be satisfied that the Conservative proposal was unreasonable. Geoffrey Lane LJ seemed to summarize the view of the Court when he said he found it 'quite impossible to say that there were any valid grounds for the Secretary of State's decision when it was given that no reasonable local authority could have acted as the borough did here'. This comes very close to an accusation of bad faith or improper purpose, that is to say that the Labour Minister, in support of a Labour policy of comprehensive schooling, was using the excuse of impracticability to promote that policy. Lord Denning MR referred to the *Padfield* decision[22] as 'a landmark in our administrative law' and applied its principles. Lord Justice Scarman put more emphasis on his view that the Secretary of State was not as fully informed as he might have been.

In the House of Lords, Lord Diplock said that the Secretary of State had to consider whether the proposal by the Conservative majority on the council would 'involve such interference with the provision of efficient instruction and training . . . that no sensible authority acting with due appreciation of its responsibilities under the Act could have decided to adopt' that course. It was, said Diplock, 'for the Secretary of State to decide that'. But he went on to conclude that there was no evidence that the Secretary of State had, in arriving at his decision, directed his mind to certain questions.

This decision takes *Padfield* one step further. It is not easy to see how the court was in a position to decide, between the Minister and the LEA, whether the Conservative proposal was or was not practicable; nor why the court should deprive the Minister of his statutory power to be satisfied that the LEA was proposing to act unreasonably. Whatever the true basis for the courts' decision it is clear that they replaced the Minister's discretionary judgment with that of their own.

Skytrain

The fifth case which illustrates judicial attitudes in the 1970s arose from the complex of decision-making powers for the granting of licences to companies to fly transatlantic passenger services. Under the Civil Aviation Act 1971, the Civil Aviation Authority was responsible for licensing in accordance with certain statutory objectives. The Act also empowered the appropriate Minister to issue 'guidance' to the CAA which was bound to perform its functions in such a manner as it considered was in accordance with that guidance. The Act also empowered the Minister to give 'directions' to the CAA for certain specified purposes.[23]

In 1971 Mr Freddie Laker applied for a licence to run a Skytrain service to the USA, in competition with British Airways and British Caledonian. The CAA granted the licence and the Minister upheld this on appeal. In 1974, the Heath Government fell and a Labour Government took office. In January 1975 the CAA refused an application by British Airways to revoke the licence but the Government refused to 'designate' Laker as a permitted carrier. The Minister in March 1976 issued a 'guidance' to the CAA stating that it should not licence more than one British airline to serve the same transatlantic route unless British Airways consented. This meant that Laker could not operate so he applied to the courts for a declaration that the 'guidance' was *ultra vires*, beyond the powers of the Ministers.

The Court of Appeal (Lord Denning MR, Roskill and Lawton L JJ) granted the declaration.[24] The Court held that 'guidance', in Denning's words, did not denote an order or command and could be used only to explain, amplify or supplement the general objectives or provisions of the statute. Because the guidance laid down 'a new policy altogether' of giving British Airways a monopoly (whereas the Act of 1971 had required the CAA to secure competition) it was invalid.

This decision is open to the criticism that it misunderstood the related functions of the CAA and the Minister; that the statute intended to put the Minister in the position of the policy-maker with the CAA as an administrative agency albeit with significant functions. The transatlantic services have inevitably been matters of international controversy and compromise and the designation of a British airline required ratification by the US Government after the US Civil Aeronautics Board had recommended the issue of a 'foreign air carrier permit'. The new Labour Government introduced a new policy at this international level. This was essentially a matter for the Government and not for the CAA. But the decision of the Court of Appeal was wholly within the Reid tradition of close scrutiny of the exercise of the discretionary powers of Ministers.

Industrial relations

The Heath Government in June 1970 inherited the legacy left by its predecessors of a failure to enact legal sanctions for the prevention or discouragement of unofficial industrial action. The trade union movement was seen as having defeated the Labour Government whose face the TUC tried unsuccessfully to save by accepting the 'solemn and binding' undertaking in 1969.

The policy of the Conservative party had developed since the Macmillan and Home administrations (1957–64) had stayed clear of conflict with the trade unions. The manifesto for the general election of 1964 promised 'an early inquiry' into the law on industrial relations. Heath's manifesto for the 1966 election promised a new Industrial Relations Act which would ensure that agreements between unions and employers were made legally enforceable, would appoint a Registrar to see that union rules were fair and in the interests of the public, would establish an Industrial Court, and would repeal the Trade Disputes Act 1965[25] to help prevent intimidation. Heath's election manifesto of 1970 added to this by promising that the new Act would lay down 'what is lawful and what is not lawful' in the conduct of industrial disputes, would provide for the holding of secret ballots, and a cooling-off period of not less than sixty days.[26]

On 2 July 1970 the Queen's speech promised that a Bill would be introduced to establish a framework of law within which improved industrial relations could develop and a code of practice would be prepared laying down standards for good management and trade union practice. On 5 April 1971 the second reading of the Industrial Relations Bill was moved in the House of Commons. It received the royal assent on 5 August 1971. The provisions of the Act were many and complex. They sought, first, to translate the agreements made locally between shop stewards and managers into legally enforceable contracts, unless the parties stated that this was not their intention. But throughout this long period of unrest in industrial relations, private-sector employers had seldom been anxious to resort to the courts to enforce discipline over their employees, believing that in the longer run this would only worsen matters. So most frequently the statement excluding legal enforceability was made by both sides. The Act provided that the trade union rules must make clear who had the authority to call a strike, or lesser action. The Act also created a large number of 'unfair industrial practices', such as inducing or threatening to induce a breach of contract or embarking on various kinds of activity supportive of other disputes, otherwise known as 'secondary' action. Powers were given to order cooling-off periods and compulsory ballots before strike action.

Trade unions were required to register but before being accepted their rules had to be approved by the Chief Registrar. These rules would, amongst other things, regulate the procedure for authorizing industrial action. Only registered trade unions would be entitled to claim those 'immunities' from civil action provided by, especially, the Trade Disputes Act of 1906.

Other advantages that accrued to registered unions were that the damages they could incur were limited to £5,000 for unions having a membership of less than 5,000, or to £100,000 for a membership of 100,000 or more. There were also tax concessions. And they could become 'sole bargaining agents'.

The structure for enforcement of these provisions included the creation of the National Industrial Relations Court (NIRC) which consisted of a judge (Sir John Donaldson) nominated by the Lord Chancellor and other members, appointed on the joint recommendation of the Lord Chancellor and the Secretary of State, having special knowledge or experience of industrial relations.

In the event, so strong was the opposition to the provisions of the Act, the great majority of the unions affiliated to the Trades

Union Congress refused to register, and so made themselves and their members liable to heavy fines and injunctions and, if they persisted in their opposition, to imprisonment for contempt of court.

Very soon, early in 1972, the NIRC faced its first test. When containers began to be used for loading goods at depots away from the docks, it was inevitable that dock workers would suffer a serious decline in available employment.[27] In Liverpool, an unofficial joint committee of shop stewards of the Transport and General Workers' Union representing docks and road haulage workers made an agreement with employers. But Heaton's Transport (St Helens) Ltd refused to sign and their lorries were blacked. The company obtained an interim order from the NIRC against the union for inducing a breach of contract between Heaton's and their customers. The union advised the joint committee to stop the blacking and, when this was ignored, the NIRC fined the union a total of £55,000.[28] This raised the question whether the union was responsible for the actions of its shop stewards. The Court of Appeal (Lord Denning MR, Buckley and Roskill L JJ) on 13 June 1972 decided it was not.[29]

At the same time, in the Port of London another shop stewards committee, acting similarly, was restrained from blacking and picketing by the NIRC which, on its own initiative, ordered the committal of three dockers to prison for contempt of court when they continued their actions. The warrants for their arrest were to be issued on 16 June. Imprisonment of trade unionists acting in defence of what they see as their rights has long been highly inflammatory, and on this occasion there was a strong likelihood of strike action on a large scale, perhaps even a general strike.

It is a common paradox that law enforcement such as imprisonment not only may fail to deter or prevent illegal acts but may stimulate them. The Government, having set up the machinery of enforcement through the NIRC, now found itself about to run into considerable political dangers as that machinery began to operate. The threatened dockers might in other circumstances have appealed against the decision to imprison them. But that would have lifted the Government off the hook on which it had impaled itself. Why should the dockers do that? But there was one official who could bring the Court of Appeal into action: the Official Solicitor. He is an officer of the court and his job is usually to represent those, like children and lunatics, who have no one to speak for them. He now asked the Court of Appeal to review the decision, although the dockers had not sought his intervention. And the Court of Appeal (Lord Denning MR, Buckley and Roskill L JJ) set aside the decision on the ground that the evidence before the NIRC had been insufficient to prove breach of the NIRC's order. The dockers were not imprisoned and the threatened strikes were averted for the time.[30]

On 3 July, the NIRC received more complaints about illegal action by seven dockers, including two of the original three and, on 21 July, committed five of the seven to prison for contempt of court. Strikes began and more were threatened. Again the Official Solicitor sought to intervene but the dockers made clear they had no intention of giving any undertakings that they would not again offend.

The impasse was formidable. There had been much talk – not least by Sir John Donaldson as president of the NIRC – about defiance of the rule of law. But the political situation was acute and dangerous for the Government. *Heaton's* case, referred to above, was quickly taken to the Law Lords who reversed the decision of the Court of Appeal and decided that the union was, after all, responsible for the actions of the shop stewards.[31] The NIRC immediately re-convened and concluded that, in those circumstances, there was no need for the dockers to remain in prison. Quite why the decision of the Law Lords in *Heaton's* case led to this conclusion was not clear, especially as the imprisoned dockers had said or done nothing to 'purge' themselves of their contempt of court (usually a necessary pre-condition of release). But the political impasse was broken.

The importance of these events was considerable. They occurred at a time when the last thing the Government wanted was a bruising encounter with the leading trade union resulting in defeat. Strikes in the coal industry in late 1971 had resulted in a state of emergency in February 1972 with much of industry reduced to a two- or three-day working week. Unemployment had risen to nearly 1 million in early 1972 but pay rises and prices were unchecked. Stagflation had arrived. Lord Wilberforce presided over an inquiry into the miners' dispute and produced a formula which resulted in a large increase in pay with *The Economist* reflecting on the device of 'calling in a High Court judge to write incredible economic nonsense'. The growth of militancy by trade unionists, with the number of days lost in strikes almost doubling in 1972, drew much of its strength from the operation of the Act of 1971 and the attempts by the NIRC to implement its provisions. Sympathetic strikes and the use of 'flying pickets' became common practice in a few of the most important industries: coal mining, the docks, car manufacturing, shipbuilding and iron and steel. Public sector employees also became more militant. Moreover, the opposition to the Act was trade union policy and led by the TUC. Previously, national trade union leaders had been to some extent marginalized by the wave of unofficial and localized strikes. Now the whole movement was drawn together and trade union membership increased annually. The jailing of the dockers had the effect of causing more unions to de-register and in 1972 the TUC suspended thirty-two small unions who had registered.

It may be that the Heath Government thought the Act of 1971 would have the effect of weakening the trade union movement when faced with the consequences of failing to register. The idea of linking registration, with its associated advantages, to acceptance of the terms of the Act was not new and in the arguments over *In Place of Strife*[32] had not been wholly rejected by the unions, so long as the penal clauses were not part of the bargain. But the full package included in the Act had the reverse effect of strengthening the unions. While this struggle was continuing, in another case the Secretary of State for Employment exercised his power under the Act to apply to the NIRC for an order requiring a ballot to be taken of the members of ASLEF before industrial action was taken. The Act provided that this power could be used where it appeared to the Minister that there were reasons for doubting whether union members wished to take the action. The union argued that there was no evidence on which it could so appear and the Minister had given no reasons for his view. The NIRC ordered that the ballot be taken and the union appealed to the Court of Appeal.[33]

Lord Denning MR stated on 19 May 1972:

> It is said that it must 'appear' to the minister that there are 'rea-
> sons' for doubting whether the workers are behind their leaders:
> and that the minister has given no reasons. We have been referred
> to several recent cases, of which *Padfield* v. *Minister of Agriculture,
> Fisheries and Food*[34] is the best example, in which the courts have
> stressed that in the ordinary way a minister should give reasons,
> and if he gives none the court may infer that he had no good
> reasons. Whilst I would apply that proposition completely in most
> cases, and particularly in cases which affect life, liberty or prop-
> erty, I do not think it applies in all cases.

And he proceeded to decide that it did not apply in this case and
that the order should stand. So it seemed that Ministers dealing
with the income of dairy farmers were required to justify their
actions but not Ministers dealing with the wages of railway workers.

Again the effect of the decision was to reinforce the long-held
view of trade unionists that they could not expect to be treated
without prejudice by the courts. When the ballot was held, 85 per
cent of those voting favoured industrial action, thus justifying the
view of many both in this country and in the USA that compulsory
ballots are at least as likely to result in increased solidarity among
trade union members as to result in division.

Industrial relations worsened. Nevertheless, as Kenneth Morgan
records,[35] in early October 1973 Labour 'looked more than ever a
nostalgic party, promising a better yesterday rather than a more
fruitful tomorrow' and the Conservative party went ahead in the
opinion polls. But there followed the fourfold increase in the
price of oil and an increase in general retail prices of 10 per cent.
The NIRC now added its contribution to the Government's
troubles.

Members of the Amalgamated Union of Engineering Workers
asked their employers to recognize the union as the sole bargaining agent for the works. When this was refused, a strike was
immediately called and backed by the union. The employers obtained an order from the NIRC declaring that this was an unfair
industrial practice under the Act of 1971. The NIRC ordered the
strike to be called off and, when this was not complied with, on

22 October found the union guilty of contempt of court and issued writs of sequestration of the union's assets in the amount of
£100,000. Later the union was fined £75,000 for its defiance.[36] A
motion was put down in the House of Commons attacking the
President of the NIRC (Sir John Donaldson).This was replied to
by the Lord Chancellor (Hailsham) in comparable terms which
resulted in a second Commons motion attacking him. The motions
were not debated.

The Heath Government now suffered its most serious, and, in
the event, fatal blow. The miners' executive had demanded large
minimum wage increases wholly inconsistent with the prices and
incomes policy which on 7 November 1973 limited increased in
pay to £2.25 per head per week or 7 per cent, and an individual
limit of £350 per year. On 12 November the miners began an
overtime ban and the Government declared a state of emergency
on 13 November, to be followed in December by a three-day
week. The minimum lending rate was raised to 13 per cent, hire
purchase controls were re-imposed and large public expenditure
cuts promised.[37] Attempts to prevent the miners' strike and other
industrial unrest continued into the new year but were unsuccessful.
On 7 February Edward Heath called a general election on the
theme of 'Who Governs Britain?' The miners' strike began on 10
February.

Throughout the period of the Heath Government, industrial
relations were the key domestic issue. The conflict between the
Government and the trade unions was sought to be resolved by
definitive rules to be enforced by the NIRC and the courts. The
attempt failed because those who were to be subjected to the
discipline were, in the circumstances of the time, too strong. Once
again it became clear that law was no substitute for politics.

The whole history of the NIRC and its relationship with the
judiciary is an example of the dangers that are involved when
judicial proceedings are invented to deal with political situations.
There is always the possibility that the orders of courts will be
defied when they are seen as appearing to subserve party political
ends. Such orders, and the laws which they enforce, may then be
viewed as unjust. And disobedience may follow. Whether such
disobedience is justified or not is always a matter for argument.

But governments are wise to seek to avoid situations which give rise to such fundamental conflicts, unless they have fully prepared both their defensive and their offensive positions.

The general election held on Thursday 28 February 1974 resulted in a hung Parliament with Labour having 301 seats, the Conservatives (including the retiring Speaker) 297, Liberals fourteen and 'others' twenty-three. After Heath had failed over the weekend to gain Liberal support, Harold Wilson became the Labour Prime Minister on 4 March. Six months later at a second election the Government won 319 seats which gave it an overall majority of three.

The Labour Government inherited the weaknesses in the economy that the Conservatives had failed to remedy and to a considerable extent their approach was, perforce, similar to that of Heath's last two years. Inflation was very high, over 20 per cent during the October election of 1974, and wage settlements were at that level also. Both increased in 1975. Labour was able to claim and to benefit from a closer relationship with the trade union leaders and a period of voluntary restraint followed in 1974–5, with the Government warning that public expenditure cuts were unavoidable. The rate of inflation fell. Soon after Wilson's retirement in March 1976, when he was succeeded by Callaghan as Prime Minister, the economic conditions worsened, as did Labour's political fortunes with by-election results having already wiped out its overall majority. Unemployment began to approach 1 million again. A run on the pound forced the Government to take a large loan from the International Monetary Fund towards the end of 1976 with consequential cuts of £2.5 billion in public expenditure over two years. The economy improved in 1977, inflation coming down to single figures and sterling strengthening. But unemployment rose to 1.6 million in September 1977. Politically, pressure was eased for the Government when a pact was entered into with the Liberals in Parliament. In 1978 the political situation worsened and those minority groups who had supported, or not opposed, the Government became less willing to do so for a variety of reasons. Prime Minister Callaghan decided against a general election in October or November and sought to impose a 5 per cent limit on wage settlements. Industrial disputes rained down on the Government during the famous 'winter of discontent' of 1978–9, and in March 1979 the Government was defeated by one vote in the Commons and resigned. At the general election, the Conservatives under Mrs Thatcher were returned with an overall majority of forty-four.

We have seen how sometimes significant litigation is triggered by governmental action or legislation. An obvious example was the exercise of powers by the NIRC under the Industrial Relations Act 1971 and the consequent appeals to the Court of Appeal and the House of Lords. At other times judicial decisions acquire importance because the courts themselves choose to interpret legislation or to apply the common law in ways which are innovative. This is what happened during the second half of the 1970s.

Very soon after the new session of Parliament was opened in March 1974, the Secretary of State for Employment (Michael Foot) introduced the Trade Union and Labour Relations Bill, the principal purpose of which was to replace the Act of 1971 and to abolish the NIRC. The provisions of the Act of 1971 concerning the Code of Practice, unfair dismissal and industrial tribunals were re-enacted. The provisions of TULRA, as it became known after its enactment on 31 July 1974, were strengthened by an amending statute in 1976.

We have seen how the Act of 1971 withheld from unregistered trade unions the protection provided by the Trade Disputes Act 1906; and how the great majority of unions decided not to register. TULRA 1974–6 restored this protection and provided in section 13 that an act done by a person in contemplation or furtherance of a trade dispute was not actionable in tort on the ground only that it induced another person to break a contract, or interfered, or induced another person to break a contract, or interfered, or induced any other person to interfere, with the performance of the contract; or threatened to induce a person to break a contract; or threatened that a contract would be broken. The section also provided that an agreement or combination to do an act in contemplation or furtherance of a trade dispute was not actionable in tort if the act, done by an individual, would not be so actionable. In 1979 Lord Scarman said, 'Briefly put, the law is now back to what Parliament had intended when it enacted the Act of 1906 but stronger and clearer than it was then.'[38] Conservative politics had sought to regulate trade union activity by law. Labour politics now removed that regulation in part. Conservative politics, as we shall see, later sought to limit that de-regulation; and then to reverse it.

Inducing breach of contract can arise in many contexts but one distinction is particularly important. A common situation, in industrial disputes, is where a member of a trade union (especially a union official) calls his fellow members out on strike. Each of those members has a legal contract of employment with their employer so the official is inducing those other members to break their contracts. Another common situation arises when, again in the course of an industrial dispute, union members bring pressure to bear on a company which has contracted to supply their employer, with goods or services on which he depends, to discontinue this supply. In the first of these examples, the inducement is to break a contract of employment; in the second, it is to break a commercial contract.

Section 3 of the Trade Disputes Act 1906 protected trade unionists from liability for breaches of contracts of employment though probably without intending impliedly to exclude commercial contracts. It was not until much later that the tort of inducing breach of contract became developed and the distinction arose between contracts of employment and commercial contracts.

Judicial development of the tort was part, indeed a leading part, of a general abandonment by the judiciary of a non-interventionist stance towards trade disputes which had characterised the four decades after 1920, an abandonment which accompanied growing governmental concern in the 1960s with increasing levels of strike activity and higher rates of inflation.[39]

In August 1976 a dispute arose between Asian employees and management at Grunwick Processing Laboratories. Strikers were sacked, union recognition refused, and mass picketing ensued in June 1977 when there were violent clashes with the police and seventy arrests. The Advisory Conciliation and Arbitration Service recommended recognition but the Court of Appeal (Lord Denning

MR, Browne and G. Lane L JJ) and the Law Lords (Diplock, Salmon, Edmund-Davies, Fraser and Keith) declared the report invalid because ACAS had not ascertained the opinions of workers to whom the issue related (as they were required to do by statute), despite the fact that they were prevented from doing so by the refusal of the management of the company to co-operate.[40] In two other cases, however, ACAS was upheld. In *UKAPE* v. *ACAS*[41] the Court of Appeal (Lord Denning MR, Lawton and Brandon L JJ) was overruled by the Law Lords (Wilberforce, Diplock, Edmund-Davies, Keith and Scarman) and in *Engineers and Managers Association* v. *ACAS*[42] the Court of Appeal (Lord Denning MR, Lawton and Cumming-Bruce L JJ) was again overruled though only by a majority (Wilberforce, Edmund-Davies and Scarman, with Diplock and Keith in the minority).

In the politics of this judicial development in the second half of the 1970s, Lord Denning MR played a considerable part. In the 1960s Denning had recognized the need to protect the right to strike and had tried to mitigate the effect of *Rookes* v. *Barnard*.[43] Also as we have seen, he held the unions not liable for the actions of shop stewards in *Heaton's* case.[44] It may be that Denning found his own balancing solution in protecting unions' rights under contracts of employment but in denying that protection where there was interference with commercial contracts. The extension of the protection to the latter was not provided until TULRA 1976 and this seems to have angered Denning and set him off on his campaign.

Everything still turned, as it had for nearly 100 years, on the statutory formula 'in contemplation or furtherance of a trade dispute', and the political as well as the judicial conflicts were now to be fought over these words and over the ways in which their application could be limited.

Between May 1977 and April 1979, the Court of Appeal, presided over by Lord Denning, gave four judgments none of which was taken to the Law Lords. Three other judgments, between December 1978 and January 1980, were reversed by the Lords who clearly felt that Denning was outrunning and disregarding his judicial superiors. The end of this sequence overlapped with the advent of the Thatcher Government and affected their legislative programme. To appreciate the attitudes of the Court of Appeal and the House of Lords it is necessary to quote at length from the judgments. Only thus can the flavours be appreciated.

The first case arose out of a proposal by the British Broadcasting Corporation to televise the Football Association cup final so that it could be seen in South Africa. Officials of the Association of Broadcasting Staff threatened to black this programme in accordance with the union's disapproval of the racial policies of the government of that country. On 20 May 1977 Denning observed that TULRA 1974–6 and the Employment Protection Act 1975 had

> conferred more freedom from restraint on trade unions than has ever been known to the law before. All legal restraints have been lifted so that they can now do as they will. Trade unions and their officers – and, indeed, groups of workmen, official or unofficial – are entitled to induce others to break their contracts – not only contracts of employment by other contracts as well – they are entitled to interfere and prevent the performance of contracts by others – all with impunity. Any such inducement or interference is not only not actionable at law. It is specifically declared to be 'not unlawful'. It is therefore proclaimed to be lawful, provided always this (and this is the one limit to the exemption which is conferred): it must be 'in contemplation or furtherance of a trade dispute.'[45]

But, said Denning, what had happened in the present case did not amount to a trade dispute between the members of the Association and the BBC. All that was happening was that the trade union, or its officers, were saying to the BBC 'Stop this televising by the Indian Ocean satellite, stop it yourself. If you don't, we will ask our own people to stop it for you.' That, said Denning, was not a trade dispute. But if the union had asked the BBC to put a clause in the contracts of employment by which union members were not bound to take part in any broadcast to South Africa and the BBC had refused, that, said Denning, would have been a trade dispute.

The next decision from the Court of Appeal was delivered six months later in November 1977. Production of the *Daily Mirror* was stopped by a journalists' dispute. As a result, the circulation of the *Daily Express* increased from 1.4 million to 2 million readers. The general secretary of the Society of Graphical and Allied Trades (SOGAT) instructed those of his members who worked for the *Daily Express* not to handle copies in excess of normal production. Denning took the view that the only trade dispute was between the *Daily Mirror* and its journalists and that the SOGAT members were not protected.[46] He said:

> The acts done were a consequence of a trade dispute, but not in 'furtherance' of it. As I read the statute [TULRA], in order that an act should be done in furtherance of a trade dispute, it must be *directly* in furtherance of it. You cannot chase consequence after consequence after consequence in a long chain and say everything that follows a trade dispute is in 'furtherance' of it.

A year later in October 1978, the Court of Appeal overturned a decision by Donaldson J who had been the president of the NIRC under the Heath Government. A bulk carrier called the *Camilla M* registered under the flag of Liberia was manned by a crew of Indian seamen at very low rates of pay. The International Transport Workers' Federation prevented her leaving Glasgow, requiring the pay to be brought up to ITWF standards. The crew refused to co-operate with the Federation and were replaced by a Grecian crew who also refused to accept ITWF terms, preferring their own articles. The Court of Appeal granted an interim injunction against the Federation. Denning said:

> It seems to me that if third persons . . . intermeddle by making threats or demands for some extraneous motive and not for any legitimate trade object, then it can be said that they are not acting in contemplation or furtherance of a trade dispute. It is suggested here that there was an extraneous motive in that they disliked flags of convenience.[47]

To understand the development of the relationship between the Court of Appeal and the Law Lords, it is best to follow the order in time in which the cases were decided in Denning's court.

Two months after the *Camilla M* case came another newspaper dispute which the Court of Appeal decided in December 1978. Journalists on provincial newspapers were in dispute over pay with their employers. To help the journalists, the NUJ called on its members at the Press Association (which supplies copy to the provincial and the national papers) to strike; about half complied. The union then instructed its members on the *Daily Express* and other nationals to refuse to use copy still supplied by the PA, and that paper sought an injunction against the members of the national executive of the union.[48] The Court of Appeal on 21 December 1978 upheld the injunction. Denning said that the only issue was whether the union's instruction to its *Daily Express* members was 'in furtherance of' a trade dispute. In his words:

It is said on behalf of the NUJ leaders that 'furtherance' depended on their state of mind. If they genuinely and honestly *believed* that the 'blacking' would advance the cause of the provincial journalists, then their acts were done 'in furtherance of' the dispute. The judge did not accept that submission. Nor do I. 'Furtherance' is not a merely subjective concept. There is an objective element in it. . . . It seems to me that, for an act to be done 'in furtherance of' a trade dispute, it must be reasonably capable of doing so, or have a reasonable prospect of it in this way, that it must help one side or the other to the dispute in a *practical* way by giving support to the one or bringing pressure to bear on the other.

In this case there is no evidence that the 'blacking' at the *Daily Express* of the Press Association copy has had any effect on the only trade dispute there is – the dispute of the provincial journalists with the local newspapers. It has had no practical effect on it at all.

In April 1979, Denning repeated his interpretation of the meaning of 'in furtherance of'. The National Graphical Association – the printers' union – were consistently refused any trade union agreement by newspaper publishers (T. Bailey Forman) and, seeking to reverse this decision, began a campaign to persuade advertisers not to insert in that newspaper by threatening the blacking of their advertisements in the national, provincial and local press. Some of those blacked sued the union. The question again was whether the union was acting in contemplation or furtherance of a trade dispute.[49]

Denning again:

> In the light of all the evidence, it seems to me that there is quite an arguable case that the dispute was not really a dispute about recognition for the purpose of collective bargaining. . . . It was a dispute in which the trade unions were determined to damage T. Bailey Forman for what the trade unions regarded as its 'anti-union' activities. . . . It could be said that they were actuated by extraneous motives and cannot rely on the Act: see *Star Sea Transport Corporation* v. *Slater*.
>
> Some acts are so remote from the trade dispute that they cannot properly be said to be 'in furtherance' of it. . . . The trade union may believe it to be in furtherance of it, but their state of mind is by no means decisive. It is the fact of 'furtherance' that matters, not the belief in it. . . . The wanton infliction of damage on innocent third persons cannot be tolerated by the law.

Now, in May 1979, came the general election, and the success of the Conservative party committed to further reform of trade union law. In June, in *NWL Ltd.* v. *Woods*, Donaldson J. granted an injunction where the facts were similar to those in *Star Sea* (see above, p. 141). But the Court of Appeal reversed him[50] saying *Star Sea* was distinguishable. In October, the Law Lords[51] upheld the Court of Appeal but overruled *Star Sea* specifically on the grounds advanced by Denning in that case. Lord Diplock said:

> If a demand on an employer by the union is about terms and conditions of employment the fact that it appears to the court to be unreasonable because compliance with it is so difficult as to be commercially impracticable or will bankrupt the employer or drive him out of business, does not prevent its being a dispute connected with terms and conditions of employment. Immunity under section 13 is not forfeited by being stubborn or pig-headed. . . . Even if the predominant object were to bring down the fabric of the present economic system by raising wages to unrealistic levels, or to drive Asian seamen from the seas except when they serve in ships beneficially owned by nationals of their own countries, this would not, in my view, make it any less a dispute connected with

terms and conditions of employment and thus a trade dispute, if the actual demand that is resisted by an employer is to the terms and conditions on which his workers are to be employed.

In late 1979, the Secretary of State for Employment (Jim Prior) was finalizing the Bill to amend trade union legislation. Because of the Court of Appeal's decision in *McShane*, he deferred a decision on whether to deal in the Bill with secondary action until after the second reading on 19 December. But on 13 December four of their Lordships (Diplock, Salmon, Keith and Scarman) explicitly rejected Denning's view that the expression 'in furtherance of a trade dispute' imported an objective test.[52] It referred, they said, to the subjective state of mind of the person doing the act and meant that he so acted with the purpose of helping parties to the dispute to achieve their objects in the honest and reasonable belief that it would do so. Lord Wilberforce preferred a rephrased objective test. He said the acts done, pursuant to the genuine intention, must be reasonably capable of achieving their objective but that it was not necessary to prove that what was done *would* achieve that objective. Lord Diplock said:

> The doer of the act may know full well that it cannot have more than a minor effect in bringing the trade dispute to the successful outcome that he favours, but nevertheless is bound to cause disastrous loss to the victim, who may be a stranger to the dispute and with no interest in its outcome. The act is none the less entitled to immunity under the section.
>
> It is, I think, these consequences of applying the subjective test that, not surprisingly, have tended to stick in judicial gorges.

But Lord Scarman was relieved to find that he was not 'called upon to review the tactics of a party to a trade dispute and to determine whether in the view of the court the tactic employed was likely to further, or advance, that party's side of the dispute'. So the Secretary of State amended his Bill to deal with secondary action.

Lord Denning was not done yet. Six weeks after this rejection by the Law Lords of his attempt to claim for the courts the power to decide whether or not the unions intended by their actions to further a trade dispute, the Court of Appeal granted an injunction against the steelworkers' union. They were on strike against their public sector employers, the British Steel Corporation. To put pressure on the Government to intervene, the union decided to extend the strike to the private sector who then sought the protection of the courts. Denning spoke of the disastrous effect this extension would have. Firms, including much of British Leyland, would have to shut down. 'Not only that, we will lose trade here in this country, and our competitors abroad will clap their hands in anticipation of being able to send their products into England because our industry is at a standstill.' Denning held that there was a second dispute, separate from that between the union and BSC. This was between the union and the Government and was not a trade dispute within the meaning of the Act entitling the union to immunity from suit. He also repeated his argument from *Wade*'s case about remoteness.[53] The Law Lords overruled the Court of Appeal on the principles they had laid down in *McShane*. Lord Diplock clearly thought that Lord Denning and the Court of Appeal were acting perversely, even defiantly.

The interaction between law and politics is nicely demonstrated by the Law Lords' rejection in *Duport Steels* v. *Sirs* of Denning's objective test. This rejection finally persuaded the Government that legislation was necessary and a new clause was added to the Bill and became section 17 of the Employment Act 1980.[54]

Lord Diplock made clear in *Duport Steels* that he profoundly disliked the provisions of the Act of 1906 and of TULRA 1974–6 which gave immunities to trade unions. The conclusion as to their 'subjective' nature was, he said, 'intrinsically repugnant to anyone who has spent his life in the practice of the law or the administration of justice'. He continued:

> Sharing those instincts it was a conclusion that I myself reached with considerable reluctance, for given the existence of a trade dispute, it involves granting to trade unions a power, which has no other limits than its own self-restraint, to inflict by means which are contrary to the general law, untold harm to industrial enterprises unconcerned with the particular dispute, to the employees of such enterprises, to members of the public and to

the nation itself, so long as those in whom the control of the trade union is vested honestly believe that to do so may assist it, albeit in a minor way, in achieving its objectives in the dispute.

But he was not prepared to give to the judiciary much latitude in interpretation in this context. Their role was 'confined to ascertaining from the words that Parliament has approved as expressing its intention what that intention was, and to giving effect to it'. And, with obvious reference to the wider role that Denning had assumed, he said it was not for the judges 'to invent fancied ambiguities as an excuse for failing to give effect to its plain meaning because they themselves consider the consequences of doing so would be inexpedient or even unjust or immoral'. He then broadened his criticism of the Court of Appeal by saying that it endangered public confidence in the political impartiality of the judiciary if judges provided 'their own preferred amendments' to statutes in the public interest.

Lord Scarman added that in developed societies limits were invariably set to the discretionary power granted to judges. 'Justice in such societies is not left to the unguided, even if experienced, sage sitting under the spreading oak tree.' The Court of Appeal had failed to construe or apply the statute in the way in which the Lords had plainly said it was to be construed and applied, and had 'strayed beyond the limits set by judicial precedent and by our (largely unwritten) Constitution'.

Retrospect

The decision in the case of the thalidomide children was one of the last handed down by Lord Reid in his long and distinguished career. He has often been praised particularly for his sense of the proper balance between Parliament, the Government, and the judiciary. There is no doubt that his judgment on these matters was informed and deepened by his political experience. But he was not noted for his particular interest in civil liberties and when faced, as in this case, with a conflict between press freedom and the protection of the process of adjudication, he seems not to have been unduly concerned at imposing prior restraint of speech in circumstances where the interference with that process was speculative and remote.

The *Hosenball* decision closed the trap more tightly for the activity there complained of by the state was, again, publication of information obtained lawfully. With the ambiguities of the *Crossman* case, these three decisions increased the likelihood of further limitations on freedom of speech in public affairs. This was to be realized in the 1980s.

The interpretations put on Ministerial powers in *Tameside* and the *Skytrain* case were further examples of the 'purposive' approach adopted by the Law Lords in the 1960s. These also presaged developments in the 1980s.

In industrial relations, the crisis developed. The failure of Labour strategy in the late 1960s was followed by the NIRC experiment which also bit the dust. Regulating the unions by new rules of law and new institutions was always likely to lead to contempt of court and, if the sanction of imprisonment were used, to serious confrontation. The Labour reforms under Wilson and then Callaghan were certainly not helped by the decisions of the Master of the Rolls in the Court of Appeal re-opening old wounds, although restrained by the Law Lords at the end of the decade.

It may be asked why the Law Lords took these steps to over-rule the Court of Appeal when they seemed to be so sympathetic to the conclusions of that Court. Those conclusions were not implausible and the statutory words could, without undue stretching, have been so interpreted by the House of Lords. Part of the answer may be that Diplock had frequently shown a greater antipathy to Denning's adventurism than had Lord Reid. Also their Lordships may have wished to avoid widening the conflict with the unions. They also knew that the Conservative Government was in the process of amending the statutes to limit the immunities of trade unions. They may have seen a future in which their 'gorges' might be unstuck and 'intrinsically repugnant' statutes repealed.

Throughout the 1970s the attitude of the judiciary significantly affected the turn of political events. The NIRC under Donaldson chose to adopt a positive and promotional role. This was not surprising as that court was created to play a crucial part in the conduct of industrial relations. When Labour changed the rules, the Government was challenged by Denning who sought so far as possible to reduce the impact of the new by re-interpreting the old legislation. But the Law Lords, perhaps seeing the political quagmire into which he might lead them, stopped on the edge just as the new Conservative Government under Mrs Thatcher began to change the rules again.

On Lord Reid's retirement in January 1975 the two senior Law Lords were Wilberforce and Diplock. They had been born in the same year, 1907, and both were Oxford men, though Wilberforce of Winchester and New College could be said (by some) to have the edge over Diplock's Whitgift and University College. Diplock became a judge (Queen's Bench Division) in 1956, was promoted to the Court of Appeal in 1961, and to the House of Lords in 1968. Wilberforce started (or chose to start) his judicial career (Chancery Division) five years later in 1961 but leapfrogged over the Court of Appeal and became a Law Lord in 1964. Wilberforce retired in 1982 and Diplock in 1985.

Both were men of great ability, both were positivists in their approach to law carrying forward the Reid tradition and the break with Simonds, neither was a civil libertarian or even a Liberal in politics, or had the abandon of Denning in his more 'creative' moments, Wilberforce indeed being inclined, in this sense, to judicial restraint. In two of the crucial cases of the 1960s, *Padfield* (1966) and *Anisminic* (1968), Diplock in the Court of Appeal was overruled by the Law Lords led by Reid (who was supported in *Anisminic* by Wilberforce).

Wilberforce gave the sole joint judgment in breaking the political impasse in *Heaton's* case in 1973; was the senior judge in *Tameside* (1976), *UKAPE* (1980) and *Express Newspapers* (1980); and crucially sided with Scarman's leading judgment in *EMA* v. *ACAS* (1980).

Diplock supported Reid in the thalidomide case (1973). He supported Wilberforce in *Tameside*, *Heaton's* case, *UKAPE*, and *Express Newspapers*. In *Grunwick* (1978), *NWL* (1979) and *Duport Steels* (1980) Diplock was the senior judge and gave the leading judgment. But where a majority of the Law Lords supported ACAS in the *EMA* case, Diplock was a dissentient.

Amongst those overlapping in membership of the House of Lords with Wilberforce and Diplock were Lord Fraser (from 1975 to 1985), Lord Keith of Kinkel (from 1976) and Lord Scarman (from 1977 to 1986). All three were Oxford men. In 1984 Fraser and Scarman became the two senior Law Lords until Keith succeeded Fraser as such in 1985.

Fraser had been a Conservative Parliamentary candidate in 1955. Keith was the son of a former Law Lord. Both were Scots and were appointed directly to the House of Lords from being Senators of the College of Justice. Scarman had been a judge of the High Court from 1961 to 1973 (chairman of the Law Commission 1965–73) and a Lord Justice of Appeal from 1973 to 1977.

Fraser and Keith supported Diplock in *Grunwick*, and *Duport Steels*. Fraser supported Diplock in *NWL*. Keith supported Scarman in *UKAPE* and *Express Newspapers* but in *EMA* he joined Diplock in dissent.

Lord Scarman had the reputation of being a liberal judge. He showed great concern about social problems, race relations, urban conflicts and poor housing. He strongly advocated the enactment of a Bill of Rights. In the Court of Appeal, he had supported Denning in the thalidomide case (1973) where the Court was overruled by the Lords; in *Tameside* (1976); and in *BBC* v. *Hearn* (1977). In the Lords he gave supporting judgments in *NWL*, *Duport Steels* and *Express Newspapers*. Most importantly, he gave the leading judgments in *UKAPE* and *EMA*.

During the 1970s, Lord Denning MR dominated the Court of Appeal. He had been appointed a High Court judge in 1944, promoted to the Court of Appeal in 1948 and became a Law Lord in 1957. In 1962, he returned to the Court of Appeal where he presided as Master of the Rolls until his retirement in 1982. During this very long career Denning exerted a strong influence over the development of English law. As we have seen he opposed the conservative and passive approach exemplified by Viscount Simonds.[55] Denning asserted the need for judges to be creative, to shape the law. Precedents were not to be followed if they seemed to work injustice. Times and circumstances changed and the courts should change with them. Inevitably Denning was seen as idiosyncratic and many of his judgments caused controversy.

In public law cases it is difficult to discover any consistency in Denning's attitudes, or any guiding principles. In *Conway* v. *Rimmer* (1967) his dissent in the Court of Appeal insisting on the right of the judges to force the disclosure of documents even in a case involving national security was upheld in the Lords. But in *Hosenball* (1977) his protection of national security was total and he found no role for the courts. In the thalidomide case (1973) Denning upheld the freedom of the press which in later cases he disregarded and then in part supported. In 1966 Denning, dissenting in the Court of Appeal in *Padfield*, strongly advocated the principle of purposive judicial review[56] and the Law Lords endorsed his view. He underlined this in *Tameside* and *Laker* (1977). But in *Aslef* (1972) he found a way to abandon the principle, when it appeared to favour the trade union. Generally in industrial relations, Denning earlier sought in *Stratford* (1964) to mitigate the impact on trade unions of *Rookes* v. *Barnard* and later to relieve them of responsibility for the actions of shop stewards in *Heaton's* case (1972). But from the mid 1970s he became the unions' chief scourge. His was a maverick and disruptive influence because so often his judgments seemed to be driven by 'visceral' emotions.[57] But there is no doubt that his long tenure as Master of the Rolls largely determined the attitudes of the Court of Appeal during the crucial middle years of the century.

Notes

1   See below, pp. 129–46.
2   *Liversidge* v. *Anderson* (see above, p. 43).
3   [1972] 3 All ER 1136, [1973] QB 710, [1974] AC 273.
4   The Insight Team of *The Sunday Times*, *Suffer the Children: The Story of Thalidomide* (1979), from which my account is drawn.
5   *Re Turner's Application* [1972] 2 QB 369.
6   [1973] 3 All ER 1136.
7   847 HC Deb. col 431–510.

8   [1973] QB 710.

9   [1974] AC 273.

10   [1982] 3 WLR 278.

11   See Hugo Young, *The Crossman Affair* (1976).

12   [1976] QB 752.

13   Cmnd 6386.

14   903 HC Deb. col *521–3* (22 January 1976).

15   194 HC Deb. col 16–17.

16   GCHQ, see below, pp. 164–8.

17   See Crispin Aubrey, *Who's Watching You?* (1981); for Home Secretary's statement see 919 HC Deb. col 1567–72 (18 November 1976).

18   926 HC Deb. col 495–507 (16 February 1977).

19   *R.* v. *Secretary of State for Home Affairs ex parte Hosenball* [1977] 1 WLR 766.

20   See above, pp. 41–3.

21   *Secretary of State for Education and Science* v. *Tameside Metropolitan Borough Council* [1976] 3 WLR 641.

22   See above, pp. 86–8.

23   See Harlow and Rawlings, *Law and Administration* (1984), pp. 52–9; and G.R. Baldwin in [1978] *Public Law* 57.

24   *Laker Airways Ltd.* v. *Department of Trade* [1977] 2 WLR 234.

25   See note 33, p. 108.

26   See F.W.S. Craig, *British General Election Manifestos 1900–1974* (1975), p. 331.

27   See Paul Davies, in 36 *Modern Law Review* (1973), p. 78.

28   *Heaton's Transport (St Helens) Ltd.* v. *TGWU* [1972] ICR 285.

29   Ibid. 308 and [1973] AC 15.

30   *Churchman* v. *Joint Shop Stewards Committee of Workers at the Port of London* [1972] 1 WLR 1094.

31   [1972] 1 ICR 308; [1973] AC 15. The Law Lords, who were unanimous, were Wilberforce, Pearson, Diplock, Cross and Salmon.

32   See above, pp. 100–1.

33   *Secretary of State for Employment* v. *Aslef* (No. 2) [1972] 2 QB 455.

34   See above, pp. 86–8.

35   Morgan, *The People's Peace* (1990), pp. 346–51.

36   *Con Mech (Engineers) Ltd.* v. *AUEW* [1973] ICR 620.

37   See Cairncross *The British Economy since 1945* (1992), pp. 198–200.

38   *NWL Ltd.* v. *Woods* [1979] ICR 867; see below, p. 143.

39   Paul Davies and Mark Freedland, in J.L. Jowell and J.P.W.B. McAuslan (eds), *Lord Denning: The Judge and the Law* (1984), p. 380.

40   *Grunwick Processing Laboratories* v. *ACAS* [1978] AC 655; and see Scarman Inquiry Cmnd 6922.

41   [1980] 1 All ER 612.

42   [1980] 1 All ER 896.

43   See above, pp. 96–8.

44   See above, p. 131.

45   *BBC* v. *Hearn* [1977] ICR 685.

46   *Beaverbrook Newspapers Ltd.* v. *Keys* [1978] ICR 582.

47   *Star Sea Transport Corporation of Monrovia* v. *Slater* [1978] IRLR 507. For interim injunctions in this and other cases, see Appendix 2.

48   *Express Newspapers* v. *McShane* [1979] ICR 210.

49   *Associated Newspaper Group* v. *Wade* [1979] ICR 664.

50   [1979] ICR 744; and see *NWL Ltd.* v. *Nelson* [1979] ICR 755.

51   [1979] 1 WLR 1294.

52   *Express Newspapers* v. *McShane* [1980] 2 WLR 89.

53   *Duport Steels Ltd.* v. *Sirs* [1980] 1 All ER 529.

54   Jim Prior, *A Balance of Power* (1986), Ch. 9.

55   See above, pp. 57–8.

56   His dissent in *Earl Fitzwilliam* (see above, p. 49) was earlier evidence of this approach.

57   See Stevens, *Law and Politics: The House of Lords as a Judicial Body 1800–1976* (1979), p. 503.

6 The Thatcher eighties

Introduction

To the general public the 1980s must have seemed like the decade when the judges came in from the cold. Some earlier cases had attracted attention, particularly the imprisonment of the dockers in 1972, the fate of the thalidomide children in 1973, the Crossman diaries in 1975, Freddie Laker and his Skytrain in 1976. But in the 1980s the courts were never out of the news. The decade was dominated, more conclusively than its immediate predecessors, by the political ideology of the time. And the attitudes adopted by the judiciary were, inevitably, reactions to this ideology reflected in the policies and in the legislation of the Thatcher administrations. Towards the end of 1981, the newly elected and Labour-controlled Greater London Council came into sharp conflict with the courts over the limits of the GLC's discretionary powers, this time challenged by a Conservative-controlled local authority. The statute was unclear and judicial interpretation became the determinant. During the first four years of the decade, a group of cases then centred on investigative journalism and press freedom, which, while not a new concern, was to become more and more important under laws which were mostly judge-made. The second half of 1984 saw the remarkable banning at GCHQ of trade union membership. This had been preceded and was to be followed by yet another string of cases on industrial relations, and the miners' strike. The years 1986 and 1987 provided first-class entertainment as the chapters of *Spycatcher* saga were written and published in serial form in different parts of the world. And, during all this, the appalling miscarriages of justice began to be revealed.

Fares fair

In 1981 the Labour party fought and won the elections to the Greater London Council on a manifesto which included a promise to reduce fares charged by the London Transport Executive on the Underground and the buses by 25 per cent. To finance this the GLC under Ken Livingstone issued a supplementary tax precept requiring all London boroughs to levy a rate of 6.1 pence in the pound. The London borough of Bromley challenged the validity of this precept.[1]

Under the Transport (London) Act 1969, the GLC was under a general duty to develop policies and to encourage, organize and, where appropriate, to carry out measures which would promote the provision of integrated, efficient and economic transport facilities and services. The GLC was authorized to make grants to the LTE for any purpose and the GLC intended by this means to reimburse the LTE for the revenue lost by the fares reduction.

The Divisional Court rejected Bromley's application but the Court of Appeal (Lord Denning MR, Watkins and Oliver L JJ) upheld it and allowed the appeal. Lord Denning was in one of his most rumbustious moods. Required to levy the additional rate, the London boroughs, said Lord Denning, 'have most reluctantly obeyed', which as a general statement was not universally true. Appeals from officers, he said, to consider the burden on ratepayers ' fell on deaf ears' and the GLC issued a press release which was 'most illuminating' in that 'it put all the blame on the Government'. The GLC decision was 'a completely uneconomic proposition done for political motives' for which there was no warrant. 'I have no doubt', said Lord Denning, that 'many ratepayers voted for the Labour party even though, on this one item alone, it was against their interest.' He realized that the decision of the Court of Appeal 'must cause much consternation to the GLC and the London Transport Executive (LTE). They will be at their wits end to know what to do. But it is their own fault. They were very foolish not to take legal advice,' and so on.

Watkins LJ for once outflanked and outbid Lord Denning. he had no doubt whatsoever that the large reduction of fares arose out of a 'hasty, ill-considered, unlawful and arbitrary use of power'.

He referred to 'the ratepayers of this great city who are unlikely to gain anything from it (many of them will in fact be at a loss)' and will bear the cost of this 'astounding' decision. The learned Lord Justice clearly could not resist the temptation to adopt the role of the political sage, for he continued:

> Those who come newly to govern people and who act in haste in wielding power to which they are unaccustomed would do well to heed the words of Gladstone. He knew a great deal about power, and in 1890 he said of it: 'The true test of a man, the test of a class, the true test of a people is power. It is when power is given into their hands that the trial comes.'

Watkins LJ called the GLC's action in implementing their policy hasty, pointing almost inevitably to 'a total lack of regard for vital legal and other considerations'. What had happened revealed 'one's worst fears of an abuse of power'. Strong words, though perhaps more to be expected from the leader of the Opposition Conservative party at the GLC than from a Lord Justice of Appeal.

Essentially, Lord Denning and Watkins LJ based those parts of their judgments where they considered the law on the proposition that the GLC were required to ensure that London Transport was run on business lines and that the granting of this large subsidy conflicted with their duty to provide 'economic' transport facilities and services.

The third member of the Court of Appeal was Oliver LJ. He based his judgment on a meticulous examination of the words of the statute. The statute required the GLC to develop policies and encourage measures which promoted the provision of integrated, efficient and economic transport facilities and services. The London Transport Executive, a creature of the GLC, was under a general duty to provide public passenger transport services which best met the needs of Greater London and to exercise and perform its functions in accordance with principles laid down by the GLC and with due regard to efficiency, economy and safety of operation. The GLC was empowered to make grants to the LTE 'for any purpose'. The LTE was required to balance its books taking one year with the next and if there was a deficit in any year the GLC could take action to remove it. Oliver LJ put overriding emphasis on this duty of the LTE to break even.

This approach was not advanced by counsel for Bromley LBC to the Court of Appeal. It was put forward by Oliver LJ himself from the bench very late in the proceedings before that court and was elaborated by him in his judgment.

The importance of Oliver LJ's judgment is that it formed the essence of the speeches of four of the Law Lords, Lord Diplock being the exception. None of their Lordships indulged in the excited politicking of Lord Denning and Watkins LJ.

The five Law Lords were Wilberforce, Diplock, Keith, Scarman and Brandon. All except Lord Diplock held that the reduction of the fares was in breach of the duty to conform to ordinary business principles; and that the GLC could not make grants to the LTE to further a particular social policy. All except Lord Keith held that the GLC had broken its fiduciary duty to its ratepayers and had unduly preferred the interests of the users of public transport. The Law Lords held that the LTE was under an obligation to balance its books taking one year with the next year and that this had to be achieved on its own internally generated income, without taking into account the GLC grant. Lord Wilberforce said:

> There is indeed, and has been for some years, discussion on the political level as to whether, and to what extent, public transport, particularly in capital cities, should be regarded, and financed, as a social service, out of taxation whether national or local. We cannot take any position in this argument: we must recognise that it exists. But I am unable to see, however carefully I re-read the 1969 Act, that Parliament had in that year taken any clear stance on it.

All this is highly reminiscent of the language and the approach of the Law Lords in the Poplar case[2] nearly sixty years previously. Here, indeed, is a wheel come full circle. A locally elected public authority, exercising wide discretionary powers, performing functions which clearly fell within its statutory jurisdiction, is held to be acting invalidly on a particular and narrow interpretation. In both cases, the policy decision of the local authorities was taken on political grounds. In both cases, the Law Lords took a different political view as the basis of their decisions. In both cases, the Law Lords favoured one group – the ratepayers – over another. In so doing the courts took on the role of political policy makers and overruled the elected body.

The policy of the Labour-controlled GLC was directed to the improvement of public transport in London at less cost to the user. This was contrary to the Conservative policies of lower public expenditure and reduced taxation. In this sense the decision of the courts could be said to reflect the spirit of the times.

The courts and the media

The relationships between the courts and the media was illustrated in four cases decided in 1980–2: *British Steel Corporation* v. *Granada Television* (1980), *Schering Chemicals Ltd.* v. *Falkman Ltd.* (1981), *Home Office* v. *Harman* (1982), *Secretary of State for Defence* v. *Guardian Newspapers* (1984).

In *BSC* v. *Granada Television*,[3] an employee of BSC, without their permission, secretly supplied Granada with confidential documents, the property of BSC. These documents were used by Granada to confront the chairman of BSC in a televised *World in Action* interview on 4 February 1980. The background was a strike of the steel workers and the main thrust of the interview was to suggest that management at BSC were at fault and that the Secretary of State for Industry (Sir Keith Joseph) had, despite Governmental denials, intervened in the dispute. Two days after the interview, BSC claimed delivery of the documents but found, on delivery, that they were mutilated to exclude internal evidence which would have identified the employee. They then required Granada to disclose his name but Granada refused. The Court of Appeal (Lord Denning MR, Templeman and Watkins L JJ) ordered this disclosure, rejecting Granada's arguments that journalists' sources ought normally to be protected and that in this case the balance of public interest lay in non-disclosure. Denning accepted the general principle and agreed that there was a balance to be struck. Newspapers, he said, should not in general be compelled to disclose sources, the public had a right to know, investigative journalism was a valuable adjunct of freedom of the press. Then, as it seemed perversely, he rejected Granada's case because, he said, they had not acted with a 'due sense of responsibility'. This turned out to mean that they had left it late in telling BSC of their intentions and did not give the chairman a chance to see the script before arriving at the studio. The conduct of the interviewer was 'deplorable' and tampering with the documents was 'disgraceful'. Denning clearly felt that Granada had pulled a fast one and not acted in a decent and gentlemanly way. Later Lord Denning wrote a number of autobiographical books and in one of them, *What Next in the Law*, revealed that he had subsequently changed his mind and thought he should have decided in favour of Granada.

Granada appealed to the Law Lords who, by a majority, dismissed their appeal. Lord Wilberforce tried to wash his hands with the extraordinary comment that 'this case does not touch upon the freedom of the press even at its periphery'. He held that the BSC had suffered 'a grievous wrong' and to deny them the opportunity of a remedy against their employee would be 'a significant denial of justice'.

Only one Law Lord dissented. Lord Salmon delivered a powerful opinion in favour of the freedom of the press. He emphasized that BSC was losing large sums of taxpayers' money and that the employee considered it his public duty to reveal the information in the documents. Lord Salmon thought that Granada were right to consider that they had a public duty to disclose any information which exposed the faults and mistakes of BSC. He concluded:

> There are no circumstances in this case which have ever before deprived or ever should deprive the press of its immunity against revealing its sources of information. The freedom of the press depends upon this immunity. Were it to disappear so would the sources from which its information is obtained; and the public be deprived of much of the information to which the public of free nation is entitled.

Schering Chemicals[4] takes us back to thalidomide country. Between 1958 and 1967 the plaintiff company Schering manufacturing and marketed the drug Primodos, used as a pregnancy test. It was suspected of causing abnormalities in newborn children and there was adverse publicity in the press (including *The Sunday Times* again) and on television. The drug was withdrawn in 1978. Schering employed the defendants Falkman Ltd to train selected executives to present Schering's point of view. In February and April 1979 Falkman held a training course for which Schering supplied information which Falkman and its instructors agreed to treat as confidential. One of the instructors conceived the idea of making a film with Thames Television and sought Schering's consent. Schering reserved their consent until they had seen the film. At about the same time (October 1979) two actions being brought by parents against Schering were set down for future trial. The film contained information supplied by Schering to the instructor who, however, claimed that he had used only material available from public sources. Schering sought an injunction to prevent the broadcasting of the film, basing its case on breach of confidence. A majority of the Court of Appeal granted the injunction.

Lord Denning MR, dissenting and speaking some nine months after his judgment in *BSC* v. *Granada*, this time came down on the side of the journalists (perhaps the doubts that were to surface later were already germinating). He founded his decision on the doctrine of prior restraint which is to say that the press must be free from censorship – 'no restraint should be placed on the press as to what they should publish'. This is a view strongly upheld in the USA as a constitutional right. What is published may be held subsequently to be illegal as being in contempt of court or defamatory or in breach of confidentiality or of the Official Secrets Acts. And the publisher or the owner or the journalist may then be liable. But the right to publish must remain intact. Even in the USA this right is not universally upheld. In the United Kingdom it is more often breached than observed as the thalidomide and *Spycatcher* cases show. 'I stand as ever for the freedom of the press, including television,' said Lord Denning invoking Blackstone's *Commentaries* (1765). Then he added, remembering his decision in *BSC* v. *Granada*, 'except when it is abused'. A principle of free speech is surely on very uncertain ground when it depends on Lord Denning's sense of abuse.

Shaw LJ for the majority had little time for these niceties. Thames TV he said were 'without any legitimate justification for canvassing the issues in flagrant breach of an elementary duty to honour confidences'. He added:

> The law of England is indeed, as Blackstone declared, a law of liberty; but the freedoms it recognises do not include a licence for the mercenary betrayal of business confidences.

The third case was *Home Office* v. *Harman.*[5] Harriet Harman, now a Labour MP, was a solicitor acting for a convicted prisoner in an action in which he was seeking to have declared illegal his detention in an experimental 'control unit'. She sought a large number of documents from the Home Office disclosing the history of these units. The department refused on the ground that it would be against the public interest for them to be made public. But a judge overruled this objection and ordered their production, it being understood (as is the general rule) that the documents would not be used for any purpose other than in connection with the case. Ms Harman was at this time also the legal officer of the National Council for Civil Liberties and she told the Treasury Solicitor that she was well aware of that rule. During the public hearing of the case a large number of these documents were read out in court.

After the hearing ended, a *Guardian* journalist asked Ms Harman if he could see those documents which had been read in open court. She allowed him to do so in her office. On 8 April 1980 the *Guardian* published an article by the journalist under the heading 'How Ministry hardliners had their way over prison units'. This referred, amongst other things, to a 'major Whitehall blunder involving internal bureaucratic intrigue and ministerial attempts to prevent disclosure'. The Home Office took proceedings against Ms Harman alleging that by allowing the journalist to see the documents she was in contempt of court. Ms Harman's defence was that what I have called 'the general rule', about the limitations attached to the use of documents obtained under the procedures governing discovery, could not apply to documents which had been read out in open court. Had the journalist taken down the words read out or had obtained a copy of the official transcript of the court proceedings, he would have been entitled to repeat those words in his article and to draw his conclusions from them. Why should the fact that he had been shown those words in the documents themselves be an offence?

Park J who first heard the case on contempt found in favour on the Home Office. 'Discovery', he said, 'is an invasion of a person's private right to keep his documents to himself.' The Court of Appeal agreed. Lord Denning MR said:

> It was in the public interest that these documents should be kept confidential. They should not be exposed to the ravages of out-siders. I regard the use made by the journalist in this case of these documents to be highly detrimental to the good ordering of soci-ety. They were used so as to launch a wholly unjustified attack on Ministers of State and high civil servants – who were only doing their very best to deal with a wicked criminal who had harassed society.

This last emphasis on the need to protect Ministers and civil servants, whom he chose to see as honest promoters of the good society, runs through many of Denning's judgments. As in *Granada*, Denning's views on 'misbehaviour' also predominate. He called Ms Harman's action 'a gross breach of the undertaking which she impliedly gave to the court and affirmed in writing to the Treasury Solicitor'. He added:

> The danger of disclosure is that critics – of one political colour or another – will seize on this confidential information so as to seek changes in governmental policy, or to condemn it. So the machin-ery of government will be hampered or even thwarted.

The case went to the House of Lords who upheld the Court of Appeal but only by the decisions of three Law Lords to two. Lord Diplock, who was joined in the majority by Lords Keith and Roskill, took a reductionist approach. First he insisted that the case was '*not* about freedom of speech, freedom of the press, openness of justice or documents coming into "public domain"'. Nor did it call for consideration of any of those human rights and fundamental freedoms in the European Convention on Human Rights. 'What this case *is* about', he said, 'is an aspect of the law of discovery of documents in civil actions in the High Court.' Like Park J he saw discovery as 'an inroad' upon the right of the individual 'to keep his own documents to himself'. Lord Keith spoke similarly of discovery constituting 'a very serious invasion of the privacy and confidentiality of a litigant's affairs'. All this applied no less, we were left to infer, when the 'individual' and the 'litigant' happened to be a Government department trying not to let a plaintiff see documents which might help his case.

Lord Scarman, who was joined in the minority by Lord Simon, dissented. Arguing that the right to receive information will generally involve a right to impart it, he said that the documents became, by production at trial, public property and public knowledge and so the journalist had a right to receive information about them and confidentiality no longer applied to them. Lord Scarman prayed in aid the European Convention and the decision of the European Court of Human Rights in the thalidomide case.

After this defeat in the Lords, the *Guardian* newspaper and the National Council for Civil Liberties took the decision to the European Commission of Human Rights, which accepted the complaint as admissible. A settlement was reached and the Rules of the Supreme Court were amended to read:

> Any undertaking, whether express or implied, not to use a document for any purposes other than those of the proceedings in which it is disclosed shall cease to apply to such document after it has been read to or by the Court, or referred to, in open court, unless the Court for special reasons has otherwise ordered on the application of a party or of the person to whom the document belongs.

The fourth case concerns the delivery in 1983 from the USA of Cruise missiles to the Royal Air Force base at Greenham Common.[6] The Secretary of State for Defence (Mr Heseltine) wrote a 'secret' minute to the Prime Minister (Mrs Thatcher) with five copies to other Ministers (including the Foreign Secretary) and one to the Secretary of the Cabinet. The minute made clear that a statement to Parliament would not be made until after the missiles had been delivered in order to minimize criticism by members of the Opposition and demonstration by protestors. Miss Tisdall, a clerk in the private office of the Foreign Secretary, disapproved strongly of this suppression of information and took photocopies of the minute which on 22 October she delivered anonymously to the *Guardian* newspaper. On 31 October the newspaper published the minute.

On 11 November the Treasury solicitor wrote to the editor of the *Guardian* asking for the return of the document and on 22 November issued a writ claiming its delivery. On 15 December Scott J so ordered and this was affirmed by the Court of Appeal the next day and complied with. Markings on the copy traced the leak to Miss Tisdall who was subsequently convicted and sentenced to six months' imprisonment.

The *Guardian*, although it had returned the document, nevertheless appealed to the House of Lords against the decision of the Court of Appeal. The basis of the appeal was section 10 of the Contempt of Court Act 1981 which provides:

> No court may require a person to disclose, nor is any person guilty of contempt of court for refusing to disclose, the source of information contained in a publication for which he is responsible, unless it be established to the satisfaction of the court that disclosure is necessary in the interests of justice or national security or for the prevention of disorder or crime.

The purpose of seeking the return of the document was to enable the Secretary of State to discover who had leaked it. Was its return 'necessary' in the interests of national security? The evidence put before the Law Lords was an affidavit sworn by the principal establishment officer of the department. All five Law Lords criticized the affidavit because it did not make clear why speedy disclosure was necessary, why there was delay between 31 October and 11 November, whether there was danger in the continued presence of whoever leaked the document. Lord Diplock thought the answers to these doubts might be inferred and that they were 'just enough' to uphold the claim that the disclosure was 'necessary'. He was supported by Lords Roskill and Bridge.

Lord Fraser took the opposite view. So did Lord Scarman who thought the evidence 'fell far short' of what was needed. 'Serious though a breach of trust by a Crown servant is', he said, 'it does not, however, necessarily follow that national security has been endangered.' So by a majority the House of Lords upheld the Court of Appeal. The decision weakens the provisions of section 10 and shows, yet again, how reluctant are the courts to uphold even statute-based protection against governmental powers when 'national security' is invoked.

Other cases followed in which the courts showed their reluctance to protect sources of information and their displeasure at investigative journalism generally. In 1986–7 the BBC programmes *Out of Court*, *The Secret Society*, *Rough Justice* and *My Country Right or Wrong* were the subject of judicial criticism or injunctions. Failures by journalists to reveal sources were punished in two recent cases.[7] And in *ex parte Brind* (1991),[8] the House of Lords upheld the Court of Appeal's refusal to review the Home Secretary's decision to ban from the BBC and independent broadcasting words spoken by representatives of legitimate political organizations in Northern Ireland. The low level of protest against these executive and judicial decisions shows the remarkable extent to which the protection of freedom of speech has ceased to be a political issue in the late twentieth century. In this case the decision of the Law Lords (Bridge, Roskill, Templeman, Ackner and Lowry) was based on the 'purposive' argument of *Padfield*, the application of *Wednesbury* principles (on this occasion to exclude judicial review), and the inapplicability of the European Convention on Human Rights.

GCHQ

This case emerged out of the decision by Prime Minister Thatcher in December 1983 (the matter did not go to Cabinet) announced by the Foreign Secretary (Sir Geoffrey Howe) on 25 January 1984 to ban civil servants at the Government Communications Headquarters (GCHQ) from membership of trade unions. Consultation with the trade unions preceding changes affecting conditions of service had been common at GCHQ. This was in accordance with the usual industrial practice. On this occasion there was no consultation, only a decision.

Between February 1979 and April 1981, the civil service staff at GCHQ was involved in industrial action, some of which resulted in some disruption, on seven occasions. Most of this action – one-day strikes, some work-to-rule and other selective action, and a protest meeting – arose from disputes not at GCHQ but on a national level over pay and conditions of service applicable to civil servants generally. Union officials claimed that at no stage was there any threat to operational capability at GCHQ. It appears that in March 1981, the then Director of GCHQ recommended the discontinuance of union membership; but no action was taken.[9] Sir Robert Armstrong, Secretary of the Cabinet and head of the civil service, said that in 1982 the Government considered the measures that could be taken to prevent such action recurring in the future. He said, notwithstanding earlier references to GCHQ in the press, 'that the disadvantages associated with the public acknowledgement of GCHQ's intelligence gathering role were a strong reason against action being taken at that time to prevent any future disruption of GCHQ's operations'.[10] So again nothing was done.

Then on 10 November 1982 Geoffrey Prime, a member of the staff at GCHQ but not a trade union member, was convicted of offences under the Official Secrets Act committed by him between 1968 and 1977 and for which he was sentenced to thirty-five years' imprisonment. The Prime Minister referred the circumstances to the Security Commission which made a number of recommendations for improving security at GCHQ, one of which was that a pilot scheme should be undertaken to test the feasibility of polygraph security screening, commonly known as the lie detector, a device to which the unions took strong exception.[11] In May and June 1983, there were meetings between union officials and Sir Robert mainly about the proposed pilot scheme. On 9 January 1984 Sir Robert wrote to the Council of Civil Service Unions promising that when the results of the pilot scheme were known, there would be further consultations. This promise was aborted by the statement of 25 January ending union membership.

Two suggestions have been frequently made to explain why the decision to ban union membership was taken. The first is that the Prime Minister was determined to introduce the polygraph lie detector and knew of union opposition to the proposal, based partly on the reported inaccuracy of the device and partly on the implicit slur on the loyalty and integrity of the staff. The second, perhaps connected, suggestion is that the Prime Minister was reacting to American pressure. 'That', said Mr Callaghan in the Commons debate, 'has been denied by the Foreign Secretary and we have to make up our own minds about that. We know that there is such a thing as deniable pressure, and I dare say there was some on this occasion.'[12] To the Select Committee, the Foreign Secretary said there was no question of American pressure but they had expressed 'understandable concern'.[13]

The civil service unions decided to challenge the legality of the decision to ban union membership and to do so without consultation. The case first came before Glidewell J in July 1984.[14] Counsel for the unions challenged the decision to ban union membership on four substantive grounds. None of these was upheld by the judge. But he did uphold the claim that the unions should have been consulted before the decision was taken. He therefore ruled, on that procedural ground, that the decision was invalid. This ruling seems to have taken counsel for the Foreign Secretary by surprise and when the case came before the Court of Appeal (Lord Lane CJ, Watkins and May L JJ) early in August, six months after the events, he advanced a new argument that consultation would itself have involved a real risk that it would occasion the very kind of disruption which was a threat to national security and which it was intended to avoid by banning union membership. The Court of Appeal, on this point, merely said that they understood the Government's anxiety that to consult might have led to disruption and doubted whether, had consultations taken place, anything useful could have been achieved. So they disagreed with Glidewell J.

The case came before the House of Lords in October and November 1984. The Law Lords agreed with Glidewell J that the staff at GCHQ had 'legitimate expectation that the Minister would consult them before issuing the instruction' and that normally the failure to do so would invalidate the Minister's decision. They then considered the Government's claim that to have consulted might have endangered national security.

They made a distinction. They accepted that only the Government could decide what national security required. The judicial process, said Lord Fraser, was 'unsuitable' for reaching decisions on national security. Lord Scarman said: 'The court will accept the opinion of the Crown or its responsible officer as to what is required to meet' the interest of national security. Lord Diplock said: 'The judicial process is totally inept to deal with the sort of problems' which national security involves. Similarly, Lord Roskill.

On the other hand, the Law Lords expressed themselves unwilling to accept without question a statement by Ministers that the interests of national security outweighed other considerations, such as the duty to act fairly, to follow the principles of national justice or, in this case, to consult. The question, said Lord Fraser, 'is one of evidence' and the government 'is under an obligation to produce evidence that the decision was in fact based on grounds of national security'. Lord Scarman said: 'Where a question as to the interest of national security arises in judicial proceedings the court has to act on evidence.' Lord Roskill said:

> The courts have long shown themselves sensitive to the assertion by the executive that considerations of national security must preclude judicial investigation of a particular individual grievance. *But even in that field* courts will not act on a mere assertion that questions of national security are involved. *Evidence* is required that the decision under challenge was in fact founded on those grounds ... *Evidence and not mere assertion must be forthcoming.* (emphasis added)

The 'evidence' was the affidavit of Sir Robert Armstrong sworn on 6 April 1984 as Secretary of the Cabinet and Head of the Home Civil Service. The crucial statement was in paragraph 16 of that affidavit. Sir Robert said:

> To have entered such consultations would have served to bring out the vulnerability of areas of operation to those who had shown themselves ready to organise disruption, and consultation with

individual members of staff at GCHQ would have been impossible without involving the national unions. Ministers also were of the view that the importance of the decision was such as to warrant its first being announced in Parliament.

The Law Lords accepted the Government's claim without explanation merely saying that there was ample evidence to support it, that it was abundantly clear, that it was compelling. Despite what they had earlier said, they proceeded more by assertion than by evidence and dismissed as 'skilful forensic play' the contention by counsel for the unions that the argument was an 'afterthought'. Earlier cases suggested that the judiciary would simply accept without question a government's claim that national security was involved and that this made unreviewable the actions of the executive. This case suggests that the judiciary will require some evidence to support the claim but that little more than a statement to that effect will suffice.

Industrial relations in the 1980s

The background to industrial relations is the state of the economy. The terms of world trade, the exchange and interest rates, the level of consumer demand, the rise and fall of wage and price inflation, all these are major determinants; so also are the personalities and ideologies of captains of industry and commerce and of trade union leaders and of the rank and file. None of these is constant, all vary amongst different groups of activities, with considerable regional variations. All act and react on one another, all being causes and effects.

Governments have the responsibility for the national economy and their success or failure will be largely assessed by the outcome of their policies. When demand is high, when living standards are rising, when unemployment is low, when social needs are being met, then governments may be content to leave well alone the negotiations between employers and employees. Between 1945 and 1960 governments intervened little. But the economic tide turned and the Labour administration of 1964–70 felt obliged to

seek to curb unofficial industrial action. This met with little success. The Heath Government fared no better with its attempts to
tighten the legal bonds around the activities of trade unions. The
second Labour Government failed to create a new consensus, and
in 1979 the Conservatives under Mrs Thatcher began their long
period of rule.

From the outset of the 1980s, as we shall see, legislation to
curb the powers of trade unions was introduced and during the
decade six major statutes were enacted. Wage inflation began to
decline during 1980. 'The interesting question', says Cairncross,
'is whether this moderation is to be attributed to labour legislation, or government pressure, or to the natural consequence of
high and rising unemployment.'[15] This last was almost certainly
the most important in the following years. In 1979 average unemployment was 1.23 million and this rose to 2.39 million in
1981, 2.98 million in 1983 and 3.35 million in September 1985.[16]
At the end of 1986 the peak was past and the total fell to perhaps
1.5 million in 1990 when it began to rise rapidly towards 3 million
again. The later figures are imprecise as comparisons because
various categories were removed from the calculations over the
period. With the increase in unemployment, membership of trade
unions declined. Unemployment apart, industrial relations were
most affected by the legislation of the 1980s, by redundancies, by
the defeats of the miners, the printers, the seamen and the dockers,
all reflecting the determination of the Thatcher Government seriously to weaken the whole trade union movement. As Hugo Young
says, 'the catastrophe of 1974 had been avenged'.[17] In these events,
the courts played an important part.

Legislation to reduce the area within which trade unions could
legally operate was the principal achievement of the Thatcher
years. A series of Acts of Parliament progressively tightened restrictions.[18] Employment Acts of 1980 and 1982 made secondary
picketing illegal, sympathy strikes actionable, and narrowed the
definition of a recognized trade dispute. The Trade Union Act
1984 required secret ballots before strikes and also for the election
of union officials. These Acts were strengthened in several ways
by the Employment Act 1988 which also greatly restricted the
operation of closed shops; and by the Employment Acts 1989 and

1990. Many other changes were introduced by or under these statutes and by other legislation such as the Public Order Act 1986, and the Wages Act 1986.

In the 1980s the senior judiciary were thus called on to interpret this legislation which, in its general purpose, was in tune with their expressed dislike of the powers of trade unions restated in the Labour legislation of the 1970s. The conflict between the trade union movement and the Government became acute during the year-long miners' strike of 1984–5.

We have already noted litigation under earlier legislation arising where the International Transport Workers' Federation sought to force shipowners to pay Federation rates of pay.[19] The Employment Act of 1980 made illegal secondary action where one person induced another to break a contract of employment with an employer who was not a party to the trade dispute. In *Marina*[20] the blacking of a ship meant that lock-keepers breached their contract with port authorities. This was held by the Court of Appeal (Lawton, Brightman and Oliver L JJ) to be illegal as there was no contract between the shipowners and the port authorities. This interpretation was confirmed two years later by the Law Lords (Diplock, Edmund-Davies, Keith, Brandon and Bright) in *Merkur*.[21]

In another case the Nottingham *Evening Post* was published by T. Bailey Foreman Ltd and printed by another company in the same group of companies called TBF (Printers) Ltd. The National Union of Journalists was in dispute with T. Bailey Foreman Ltd and boycotted all work with the group. Dimbleby and Sons published local papers in London and were in dispute with the National Graphical Association (the printing union), so instead they contracted with TBF (Printers) Ltd. The NUJ told its members not to submit any copy to be printed by TBF (Printers) Ltd. They obeyed and were suspended. Dimbleby brought an action against the NUJ for an injunction.[22] The Court of Appeal (Donaldson MR, Griffiths and Stephen Brown L JJ) upheld the grant of the injunction as did the House of Lords (Diplock, Fraser, Scarman, Bridge and Brandon) on the ground that the only protected trade dispute was between the NUJ and T. Bailey Foreman Ltd, that TBF (Printers) Ltd were separate from T. Bailey Foreman

Ltd, and that there was no contract between T. Bailey Foreman Ltd and Dimbleby and Sons. As McIlroy says: 'This case illustrated the opportunities open to employers to reorganise their operations and manipulate company structures to outlaw secondary action in industrial disputes.'[23] And the judges took the view that, for the purposes of this legislation, different companies were to be treated as separate persons although they were, in reality, closely linked and interdependent.

In 1983 and 1984 the High Court gave judgments on the 'Eddie Shah' case. When six NGA members at the *Messenger* newspaper at Stockton were dismissed, the union picketed Shah's plants at Bury and Warrington and sought to black all *Messenger* newspapers and dissuade advertisers from using them. In October 1983 Shah obtained injunctions against the NGA and the NUJ to stop secondary picketing and the enforcement of 100 per cent union membership. The NGA did not comply, were found to be in contempt of court and fined £150,000. Mass picketing and violence continued, the police were deployed in large numbers, and the union's assets were sequestrated and a further £525,000 fines plus damages exceeding £125,000 were imposed.[24] In the event the General Council of the TUC was not prepared to give practical support by action in such circumstances.

These cases set the scene for the conflicts that were to mark the 1980s, involving the Thatcher Government, the unions and the courts. Most significant was the enforcement, by way of contempt of court, for failure to obey injunctions, followed by heavy fining, and, above all, the sequestration of assets which threatened the existence of unions if they did not comply.

The significance of changes in the wording of the law is shown in the *Mercury* case.[25] In TULRA 1974–6,[26] 'trade dispute' was defined as a dispute between employers and workers, or between workers and workers, which was 'connected with' one or more matters including terms and conditions of employment. In *NWL* v. *Woods* (1979)[27] the Law Lords found for the union on this basis. The Employment Act 1982 changed the wording and provided that for a trade dispute to be protected it had to be 'wholly or mainly' about the specified matters. The Post Office Engineering Union instructed its members not to connect the new company

Mercury to the British Telecom network, partly because it feared loss of jobs for its members. But the Court of Appeal (Lord Donaldson, May and Dillon L JJ) decided that the dispute was 'mainly' about the Government's privatization policy, to which the union was opposed, and was therefore a political not an industrial dispute. Distinguishing these two motivations is difficult enough. To require judges to determine which predominated during a period of high unemployment was to require them to embark on overt political analysis. The application by Mercury was for an interim injunction and the court decided at this stage that there was 'a serious question to be tried' and that the balance of convenience lay in protecting Mercury, pending the trial of the action.[28] The burden of proving that the motivation was not 'political' was impossibly heavy, especially as Lord Donaldson took the view that the new definition was meant to be 'relatively restrictive'.

In March 1984, the miners's strike began.[29] Picketing was widespread and clashes with the police were often fierce. McIlroy records that 9,808 people were arrested in England and Wales (80 per cent were charged) and 1,483 in Scotland (57 per cent charged). The great majority of the charges were for minor offences and heard in magistrates' courts.[30] In the High Court the setting up by the police of road blocks some distance away from pitheads to prevent picketing was upheld;[31] so was the imposition of restrictive bail conditions. The National Union of Mineworkers in another case was fined £200,000 with sequestration of assets[32] and the South Wales area of the union £50,000 backed with heavy sequestration of funds.[33] Amongst the many reasons for the defeat of the miners' strike, the use of these financial penalties was one of the most potent.

The turbulent 1980s continued with the opposition, mostly by the Society of Graphical and Allied Trades and the NGA, to Rupert Murdoch's proposal to transfer the production of the *Sun*, the *News of the World*, *The Times* and the *Sunday Times* to Wapping. The unions in autumn 1985 were faced with new terms and conditions of work. In January 1986 the strike began, followed by the dismissal of 5,000 printers and journalists who had refused to move. Heavy picketing was started at Wapping and the police attended in force. Injunctions were obtained against SOGAT, the NGA and other unions mainly on the ground of secondary action and failure to conduct strike ballots. In February 1986, SOGAT was fined £¼ million with sequestration for failing to obey an injunction and NGA £25,000. In July 1986 SOGAT was ordered to stop picketing and in January 1987, when threatened with contempt proceedings, withdrew support for the strike.[34]

The principal reason why the Murdoch newspapers succeeded in defeating the unions was that the legislation of the early 1980s provided all the weapons needed for that purpose. In addition, the trade union movement was split with the EETPU and some members of the NUJ continuing to work at Wapping. Thirdly, and this applies to other disputes also, the courts, faced with failure or refusal to comply with injunctions, were prepared to impose massive fines and to support these with sequestration of assets and the appointment of receivers. Given the expressed distaste of the most senior judges for Labour legislation of the 1970s restoring some protection to the unions, it is not surprising that their attitude to the Conservative legislation of the 1980s was highly supportive of the Government.

Various attempts, some successful, were made to persuade the courts that unions had not complied with the requirements for holding ballots before strikes. The Employment Act 1988 tightened the requirement.

In 1988 a major dispute arose between the National Union of Seamen and the shipping companies over terms and conditions of work. A Sealink subsidiary company dismissed sixteen striking seamen and on 30 January the NUS called a national strike in their support and because similar dismissals were expected by the shipping companies (P & O and Sealink). But the courts saw the NUS action as 'secondary' and illegal and granted an injunction. The union called off the strike but many thousands stayed out and the NUS was fined £7,500 for contempt. By now over 2,000 striking workers had been dismissed and the NUS prepared to ballot all their members. P & O then persuaded the judge (Michael Davies J) to grant an injunction prohibiting the NUS from holding a ballot on the ground that a strike authorized by the ballot would be illegal as secondary action. Union members stayed out and on

3 May the NUS was fined £150,000 plus sequestration of £2.8 million assets and other penalties. On 11 May, a further fine of £150,000 was imposed with threats of more to follow. The NUS ordered its members to return to work but mass picketing continued at Dover. More fines followed. McIlroy estimates that eventually when the sequestration order was lifted the NUS was liable for fines of £350,000 and legal costs at over £900,000.[35] The strike at Dover ended on 9 June 1989 having lasted for sixteen months.

In the summer of 1989, two cases intertwined with curious results. The National Union of Railwaymen called for a strike, after being strongly supported in a ballot, to begin at midnight on 7 May. But on 4 May the employers (London Underground) were granted an injunction on the ground that the question on the ballot paper might be held to include matters which were not trade disputes.[36] The NUR took another ballot, this time of all its members and again obtained, on 13 June, a substantial majority for industrial action. A twenty-four-hour stoppage was called for 21 June. The employers (British Railways) sought an injunction on 18 June, arguing that the ballot had been improperly conducted. This was refused by the High Court. BR appealed and were heard the next day by the Court of Appeal (Lord Donaldson MR, Butler-Sloss and Stuart-Smith L JJ) which dismissed their appeal.[37] 'In my judgment', said Lord Donaldson, 'it is in highest degree likely that the NUR would at the trial of the action establish the matters which . . . would afford a defence to any action against them.'

The other major case of 1989 concerned the statutory national Dock Labour Scheme. This was first introduced in 1947 to end casualization of labour and to provide some permanency of employment to those registered as dock workers. Certain ports were outside the scheme. The Conservative Government had for some time been under pressure to end the Scheme and in 1988 disputes arose when some employers refused to use registered dockers, with the result that dock workers' delegates to a conference of Transport and General Workers called for a ballot for a strike.

On 7 April 1989 the Government issued a White Paper and a Bill to abolish the Scheme. The T & GWU on 20 April announced a strike ballot on the question of terms and conditions of employment (to avoid falling into the *Mercury* trap of having the strike designated by the courts as 'political' and so illegal). On 8 May the employers sought an injunction on the ground that no genuine trade dispute existed and that a strike would be in breach of the Scheme. On 19 May the ballot resulted in a three to one majority for industrial action and on 27 May the High Court held that the dispute was valid and that the employers had negligible prospects of showing that the strike was unlawful.[38]

In the meantime the Bill abolishing the Scheme was being pushed through Parliament having received its second reading in the House of Commons on 17 April. Before the Court of Appeal, however, the employers argued that since, under clause 8(5)(b) of the Scheme, each registered docker was required to 'work for such periods as are reasonable in his particular case', any withdrawal of labour was in breach of this statutory duty. This remarkable proposition, which meant that registered dockers, and any other workers employed under a similar provision, had never been entitled legally to withhold their labour, was accepted by 7 June by the Court of Appeal (Neill, Butler-Sloss and Stuart-Smith L JJ). The Court further held that an interim injunction should issue because a strike would damage the economic well-being of the nation.

No date for the hearing of the appeal to the Law Lords having been given, some dockers walked out from 9 June. On 21 June, Lords Bridge, Roskill, Ackner, Goff and Lowry overruled the Court of Appeal on the ground that the obligation of registered dock workers was contractual, the provisions as to periods of work being regulated primarily by national or local agreements, and that clause 8(5)(b) imposed no additional statutory obligation to work.[39] On 3 July the Dock Work Bill received the Royal Assent and the Scheme came to an end. On 8 July an official strike began but collapsed within weeks.

Spycatcher

The most notorious of the cases in the 1980s were those in which the Government sought to prevent the national press from publishing extracts from Peter Wright's *Spycatcher*. He had been a member of the internal security service known as MI5 from 1955 to 1976 and these were his memoirs. First, the Attorney-General of the United Kingdom sought in Australia to restrain publication of the book on the ground that the material was confidential and that Wright was bound by the terms of his employment and the Official Secrets Acts not to disclose it. In June 1986, while the Australian proceedings were progressing, the *Guardian* and the *Observer* published articles outlining allegations made in *Spycatcher*. On 11 July 1986, Millett J granted the Attorney-General an injunction, pending the full-trial, preventing those newspapers from making further publication. On 25 July the Court of Appeal (Donaldson MR, Mustill and Nourse L JJ) upheld this decision.[40]

In mid July 1987 the *Sunday Times* published extracts from *Spycatcher* and the book was published in the USA, the proceedings to prevent publication in Australia having failed. The *Guardian* and the *Observer* now sought to have the Millett injunction discharged and this was agreed by the Chancery Division on 22 July. The Vice-Chancellor said:

If the courts were to make orders manifestly incapable of achieving their avowed purpose, such as to prevent the dissemination of information which is already disseminated the law would to my mind indeed be an ass.

Undeterred by this prospect, the Court of Appeal reinstated the injunction in an amended form.[41] Sir John Donaldson MR said:

I accept that to the extent that these publications have been read, the information to which they relate has become public knowledge, but not that it has entered the public domain, so losing the seal of confidentiality, because that only occurs when information not only becomes a matter of public knowledge, but also public property.

On 13 August 1987, the House of Lords gave the crucial judgment of the saga.[42] The book was now available in the United Kingdom for anyone who wished to obtain a copy, no attempt having been made to prevent its importation from the USA or elsewhere. But the Government, in the person of the Attorney-

General, was still determined to get the ruling it sought even if (one must assume) this did result in the law being made to look an ass. Under this strain their Lordships divided 3–2, the majority (Lords Brandon, Templeman and Ackner) supporting the Government's claim though emphasizing that the full trial was still to come when the injunction might be set aside.

Lord Oliver dissented saying that he could not but feel that their Lordships were being asked to beat the air and to interfere with an essential freedom for the preservation of a confidentiality that had already been lost beyond recall.

Lord Bridge was the other dissentient. He used the strongest words heard from the House of Lords since Lord Atkin in *Liversidge* v. *Anderson*:

> Freedom of speech is always the first casualty under a totalitarian regime. Such a regime cannot afford to allow the free circulation of information and ideas to regulate what the public may and what they may not know. The present attempt to insulate the public in this country from information which is freely available elsewhere is a significant step down that very dangerous road.

By this time the Government was beginning to look ridiculous and the senior judiciary absurd. What kind of a system was this under which injunctions were upheld to prevent the newspaper publication of material easily available in book form? The Court of Appeal, led by the Master of the Rolls, and supported by a majority of the Law Lords seemed to be intent on assisting the Government's heavy pursuit of a quarry who had long escaped into the open spaces and was now beyond capture. The pursuit seemed to be driven by a Prime Minister angered by the indiscreet revelations[43] of a former civil servant who had chosen to depart from the traditions of the service (not that he was alone in this) and to break confidences.

One explanation of the attitude of the majority of the judges who took part in this process is that they saw the issue as being one, however remotely, of national security. But Peter Wright's disclosures (none of which was less than ten years old) offered no contemporary threat. Perhaps they thought he should not be allowed to escape the consequences of his actions – and incidentally make a considerable financial profit. If there was this element of discouraging others, it is doubtful if the outcome aided the cause.

The dénouement came when in November and December 1987 the full trial eventually began to be heard. Scott J at the end of a long judgment refused injunctive relief. The Court of Appeal[44] and the Law Lords agreed in substance.[45] Lord Keith may have the last word:

> A communication about some aspect of government activity which does no harm to the interests of the nation cannot, even where the original disclosure has been made in breach of confidence, be restrained on the ground of a nebulous equitable duty of conscience serving no useful practical purpose.

The *Observer* and the *Guardian* took their case to the European Court of Human Rights, arguing that the imposing of the injunctions was contrary to Article 10 of the Convention, protecting freedom of expression. As is usual in these cases the Government argued that the injunctions were, in the words of the Convention, 'necessary in a democratic society'. To the dismay of civil libertarians, a majority of the Court found that the original injunctions granted by Millett J did not infringe the article, though their continuance, after the publication of *Spycatcher* in the USA, did so infringe.[46] Once again the European Court of Human Rights failed to present an unambiguous defence of free speech.

Miscarriages of justice

A jury arriving at a decision to convict, which subsequently turns out to be unsafe or unsatisfactory, may have been misled by the evidence put before it, or by evidence withheld or not disclosed, or by the judge's summing up. None of this has, in generally, much to do with judicial attitudes though the approach of individual judges has been criticized. But attitudes are revealed by statements made by judges when asked to review convictions on which doubt has been cast. Until very recently the courts have been most reluctant to overturn such decisions, as if they thought that the result of their doing so would weaken the public's confidence in the whole judicial process and that this must be avoided even at the cost of upholding a wrongful conviction. It also seems that the Court of Appeal is not an efficient body to carry out a review. This is evidenced by the statement of the Court in the case of the Birmingham Six when Lord Lane CJ said in January 1988: 'The longer the hearing has gone on the more convinced this Court has become that the verdict of the jury was correct. We have no doubt that these convictions were both safe and satisfactory.' In March 1991, after further investigations, the Six were set free. Earlier there had been the notorious statement by Lord Denning when he contemplated the possibility, of the Six succeeding in a civil action against the police for injuries they claimed to have received while in custody. This, involving as it would the police being found guilty, of perjury, of violence and of threats, involuntary confessions having been improperly admitted in evidence, resulting in erroneous convictions, Lord Denning called 'such as appalling vista' that the action should not be allowed to go further.[47]

The weight of so many miscarriages is likely to bring about changes in the procedures after the report of the Royal Commission in 1993.

Retrospect

The *Bromley* decision continued and re-inforced the activist approach begun in the 1960s. In earlier decades, at least lip service would have been paid to the principle that where Parliament had conferred discretionary powers on public authorities – especially those elected – the courts would be most reluctant to intervene when to do so meant that the exercise of the discretion passed away from the statutory body and to the judiciary. Moreover the facts of this case showed clearly that the political philosophy of the country's most important metropolitan authority was in opposition to that of the central Government. So the decision did serious damage to the tradition of local autonomy and led to the dissolution of the GLC and the general weakening of local government. How far the courts realized that these were natural consequences we cannot say but the case remains one of the most significant political actions of the judiciary since 1945.

The media cases illustrate judicial attitudes both to the media and more widely. Public authorities are to be protected from criticism and this is particularly so when the media are seen as acting 'unfairly', or 'abusing' their powers, or indulging in 'misbehaviour'. Ministers and public servants are regarded as decent chaps doing their best in difficult situations and so to be shielded from dirty tricks like using documents leaked to them or enabling journalists to write articles revealing governmental shortcomings. Ringing declarations of principle supporting freedom of expression may be followed by particular reasons justifying the protection of special interests. The protection of private property rights has long been a prime concern of the common law. Business and commercial confidences must be preserved and discovery of documents is seen as an invasion of those rights. Questions of general importance may be subordinated to such interests. Judges dealing with what look to the outside world as matters affecting freedom of speech (as in the *Granada*, *Harman* and *Guardian* cases) testily deny that this is so. When individual judges are prepared to decide on the basis of the wider issues (Lord Salmon in *Granada*; Lord Denning in *Schering*; Lords Scarman and Simon in *Harman*) they are overruled. The general pattern repeated again and again through the cases is of the senior judiciary not being willing to support those forces in the media who regard their function as subjecting the actions of public authorities to critical scrutiny.

The arbitrary ban on trade union membership by the Prime Minister and the Foreign Secretary was an extraordinary political act. The right of association had been fought for and won more than 150 years previously. The ban would have been unthinkable to Mrs Thatcher's first Secretary of State for Employment. Indeed Mr Prior later called it insensitive and said the failure to consult was incredible: 'Even the most rabid right-wingers in the union movement were appalled.' He added that the rejection of the union's offer of a no-strike agreement was 'an act of further stupidity'.[48] The *Daily Telegraph* described the behaviour of

Ministers as 'little short of shambolic' and the *Daily Express* described the decision as 'highly illiberal and authoritarian'.[49]

Mrs Thatcher's biographer attributes the decision itself, and the refusal on the part of the Government to compromise, wholly to the Prime Minister personally, backed by her Press Secretary Bernard Ingham and her Private Secretary Robin Butler (now the Secretary to the Cabinet and head of the civil service.)[50]

Perhaps in another country in another time – possibly the Supreme Court of the USA during one of its independent moods – the judiciary might have struck down the decision and insisted, as did Glidewell J, on the right of the union to be consulted. But no one among the eight judges in the Court of Appeal and the House of Lords was willing or even, it would seem, interested in making such a stand.

The attitude of the courts to the Conservative legislation on trade unions during the 1980s was predictable. The disclosed distaste for the Labour legislation of the 1970s which resulted in the decisions of the Court of Appeal under Denning, tempered towards the end of the decade by the reluctant acceptance by the Law Lords of the intentions of that legislation, resulted in a willingness to implement and, on some occasions, to push further the statutes of 1980, 1982, 1984 and 1988. No doubt, as Donaldson said of the 1982 Act, this legislation was meant to be 'relatively restrictive', an interpretation which covers a wide range of meaning. The distinction drawn between 'political' and 'industrial' action, the insistence on the formal difference as legal persons between companies of the same group, the use of sequestration and the appointment of receivers to impose heavy fines while avoiding the imprisonment of those responsible for contempt of court, all these undoubtedly flowed from the legislation and were applied in ways which subjected the unions to close discipline. But the willingness to prevent a strike ballot from taking place and the extraordinary decision of the Court of Appeal to deny the right to strike under the Dock Labour Scheme pushed the implementation of the anti-union spirit of the times beyond acceptable limits so that in the second of these cases the Law Lords had to call a halt in a way reminiscent of their rejection of Denning's re-interpretation of the law in the late 1970s.

No one can doubt that Mrs Thatcher was the driving power behind the *Spycatcher* litigation. In her later years she seemed to lose her talent for spotting a loser and allowed her passion to override her judgment. Some of the responsibility for allowing the campaign to continue must lie with the Court of Appeal, but the main blame must be carried by the three Law Lords who persisted during the summer of 1987 even in the face of dissent of two of their colleagues as distinguished as Lords Bridge and Oliver.

Before retiring in March 1982, Lord Wilberforce presided as senior Law Lord in *BSC* v. *Granada* (1980) and *Bromley* v. *GLC* (1981) in both of which he delivered full judgments. The serious nature of the *BSC* decision was emphasized by the dissent of Lord Salmon who had been a High Court judge from 1957 to 1964, then a Lord Justice until 1972 when he was appointed a Law Lord. He said: 'There are no circumstances in this case which have ever before deprived or ever should deprive the press of its immunity against revealing its sources of information', but, as we have seen, such judicial advocacy for freedom of speech has become unusual in recent years.

Lord Diplock relinquished his position as a senior Law Lord in 1984 but continued to sit until his death the following year. He delivered a full judgment in *Bromley* and led the majority in *Home Office* v. *Harman* (1982). In the two important trade union decisions of *Merkur* (1983) and *Dimbleby* (1984), Diplock spoke for all their Lordships. In *Defence Secretary* v. *Guardian* (1984) he again led the majority as senior Law Lord, this time in the face of dissents from Lords Fraser and Scarman. In the *GCHQ* case (1984) he fully supported Fraser's leading judgment. Lord Fraser in addition to these two judgments supported Wilberforce in *BSC* v. *Granada* and concurred with Diplock in *Dimbleby*.

Scarman now joined Fraser as senior Law Lord. He had disappointed those who looked to him as a liberal judge by his support for his colleagues in *Bromley* and *GCHQ*. It was less surprising that he should support Diplock in *Dimbleby*, and the liberals were heartened by his dissents in *Harman* and the *Guardian* case.

On Fraser's retirement, Lord Keith became a senior Law Lord in 1985, a position he was still holding at the end of the decade.

He participated in the unanimous decisions of *Bromley* and *Merkur*, and was with the majority in *Harman*. In October 1988 he presided over an Appellate Committee most of whom had been recently appointed as Law Lords: Brightman (1982), Griffiths (1985), Goff (1986) and Jauncey (1988). They applied the *coup de grâce* to the *Spycatcher* litigation. In the previous hearing in August 1987, when a majority of the Law Lords had decided to continue the injunctions, Lord Bridge, a senior Law Lord, made his strong dissent (supported by Lord Oliver). He also presided in *Associated British Ports* v. *TGWU* (1989) and *ex parte Brind* (1991).

At the beginning of the 1980s, Lord Denning was still Master of the Rolls. He granted the injunction in *BSC* v. *Granada* (1980), supported by Templeman and Watkins L JJ; allowed *Bromley's* appeal (1981) with Watkins and Oliver L JJ; and upheld the finding of contempt in *Harman* (1981) with Templeman and Dunn L JJ. These three decisions were confirmed by the Law Lords. *Schering's* case (1981) was one of the very few cases when Denning was in a minority in his court. He would have refused the injunction and upheld the broadcast but had to yield to the views of Shaw and Templeman L JJ. The case was not taken to the Lords.

In 1982 Lord Denning finally retired from the bench in his eighty-fourth year, after voicing one of the remarks (in this instance about the racial composition of a jury) for which he had become notorious. He was succeeded as Master of the Rolls and president of the Court of Appeal by Lord Donaldson (as he became) who retired in 1992. Donaldson was a Cambridge man, had seen war service, served as a Conservative county borough councillor from 1949 to 1953 and became a High Court judge in 1966. As we have seen he was appointed by the Heath administration to lead the National Industrial Relations Court from 1971 to 1974.[51] In 1979 he was appointed by Mrs Thatcher to the Court of Appeal. Because of his presidency of the NIRC, Donaldson was a minor member of Labour's demonology and had reputedly been denied judicial promotion during the Wilson and Callaghan administrations 1974 to 1979.

In the trade union cases of *Merkur* (1983) and *Dimbleby* (1984), the Court of Appeal under Donaldson was upheld in the Lords; in *Mercury* (1983) and *BR* v. *NUR* (1989) the Court's decisions were not appealed. In *Defence Secretary* v. *Guardian* (1983) and in *Brind* (1989) the Court's decision were upheld. In these six cases, Donaldson was supported by ten different Lord Justices, none of whom dissented. But Donaldson's most important involvement was in the four *Spycatcher* decisions. As we have seen, the Court of Appeal under his presidency rejected the appeal against the Millett injunction; reversed the Vice-Chancellor's finding for the *Independent* and, later, for the *Guardian* and the *Observer*; Donaldson and Bingham entered partial dissents when allowing the final appeal.

Spycatcher provided a highly controversial set of judgments. In retrospect, Lord Donaldson MR emerged with little credit and could have prevented the ridicule which the cases brought on to the senior judiciary. In particular his attempt to continue the injunctions by seeking to modify that granted originally by Millett J was rejected as unworkable by all parties. The Master of the Rolls gave the impression of trying to find a practical solution which would satisfy both sides without realizing that this course would debase not merely the Government but the judicial process itself. Nevertheless his continuance of the injunctions was substantially supported by a majority of the Law Lords in the third and critical case so that the final responsibility for the débâcle must rest with Lords Brandon, Templeman and Ackner.

Notes

1   *Bromley LBC* v. *Greater London Council* [1983] 1 AC 768.
2   *Roberts* v. *Hopwood* [1925] AC 578, see above, pp. 7–11.
3   [1980] 3 WLR 774.
4   [1982] QB 1.
5   [1981] 2 WLR 310; [1983] 1 AC 280.
6   *Secretary of State for Defence* v. *Guardian Newspapers* [1984] 3 WLR 986.
7   *Re an Inquiry under the Company Securities (Insider Dealing) Act 1985* [1988] 2 WLR 33 and *X Ltd.* v. *Morgan Grampian (Publishers) Ltd.* [1990] 2 WLR 1000.
8   [1991] 2 WLR 588.
9   See First Report of the Employment Committee HC 238 of 1983–4, Q.157.

10   First affidavit, para. 11, quoted by Glidewell J in the Queen's Bench Division on 16 July 1984.

11   Cmnd 8876.

12   55 HC Deb. col 47.

13   HC 238 of 1983–4, Q.90, 130 and 211.

14   *Council of Civil Service Unions* v. *Minister for the Civil Service* [1984] 3 All ER 935.

15   Cairncross, *The British Economy since 1945* (1992), p. 255.

16   Key Data 1986 (CSO 1986 London), p. 14, quoted by Coates, *The Crisis of Labour* (1989), p. 126.

17   *One of Us* (1989), pp. 376–7.

18   Apart from the standard works on trade union law, see especially David Coates, *The Crisis of Labour* (1989) and John McIlroy, *The Permanent Revolution?* (1991), to both of which I am indebted.

19   See *Star Sea Transport* (1978) above, p. 141.

20   *Marina Shipping Ltd.* v. *Laughton* [1982] 2 WLR 569.

21   *Merkur* v. *Island Shipping Corporation* v. *Laughton* [1983] 2 All ER 189.

22   *Dimbleby and Sons Ltd* v. *National Union of Journalists* [1984] 1 WLR 427.

23   McIlroy, *The Permanent Revolution?* (1991), p. 76.

24   *Messenger Newspapers* v. *NGA* [1984] IRLR 397.

25   *Mercury Communications Ltd.* v. *Scott-Garner* [1984] Ch. 37.

26   See above, p. 137.

27   See above, p. 143.

28   See Appendix 2, p. 194.

29   See M. Adeney and J. Lloyd, *The Miners' Strike* (1986).

30   McIlroy, *The Permanent Revolution?* (1991), p. 89.

31   *Moss* v. *McLachlan* [1985] IRLR 76.

32   *Clarke* v. *Heathfield* [1985] ICR 203 and (No. 2) at 606.

33   *Read (Transport) Ltd.* v. *NUM (South Wales Area)* [1985] IRLR 136; J. McIlroy, in Bob Fine and Robert Millar (eds), *Policing the Miners' Strike* (1985), pp. 88–9.

34   *News Group Newspapers* v. *Sogat* [1986] IRLR 227, 337.

35   McIlroy, *The Permanent Revolution?* (1991), p. 148; *P & O European Ferries (Portsmouth)* v. *NUS* (1988).

36   *London Underground Ltd.* v. *NUR* [1989] IRLR 341.

37   *British Railways Board* v. *NUR* [1989] IRLR 345, 349.

38   *Associated British Ports* v. *Transport and General Workers' Union* [1989] IRLR 291.

39   [1989] 1 WLR 939.

40   *Att-Gen* v. *Guardian Newspapers and others* [1989] 2 Fleet Street
      Reports 3.
41   [1987] IWLR 1248.
42   [1987] IWLR 1282.
43   See Hugo Young, *One of Us* (1989), pp. 461–3.
44   [1988] 2 WLR 805; Donaldson MR, Dillon and Bingham L JJ.
45   [1988] 3 WLR 776; Lords Keith, Brightman, Griffiths, Goff and
      Jauncey, none of whom had sat on the case before.
46   See Ian Leigh, 'Spycatcher in Strasbourg', in [1992] *Public Law*,
      p. 200.
47   See Chris Mullin, *Error of Judgement* (1990), p. 216.
48   Jim Prior, *A Balance of Power* (1986), p. 256.
49   *Per* D. Healey MP at 55 HC Deb. col 35 (27 February 1984).
50   Hugo Young, *One of Us* (1989), p. 356.
51   See above, p. 130.

7 Retrospect

Under our system of public law, the courts are required to consider whether public bodies (which includes combinations of employers and employees) have acted within the law. But this is an exercise of much complexity because those bodies rarely act in ways which are consciously or blatantly illegal. Ministers, local authorities, public servants, companies and trade unions seek to promote their own interests within the powers they have and this often brings them into conflict with other interests, including individuals who see themselves as disadvantaged by the exercise of those powers. And disputes arise on which the courts must adjudicate.

Rules of law are general statements about powers and, being general, are inevitably imprecise and call for interpretation. We saw a simple example of this in the Poplar case of *Roberts* v. *Hopwood*. Had the local councillors exceeded their wage-fixing powers? What were the limits of those powers? We saw how two of the most eminent judges, in the Court of Appeal, came to a decision in favour of the local authority and how five judges in the House of Lords, some of them deciding on quite different grounds, came to the opposite conclusion. But, as importantly, we also saw the emergence of some criteria for the adjudications, some judge-made principles of statutory interpretation. Moreover this decision and these criteria were not remote activities, games being played in wigs and gowns in mahogany courtrooms, but had historical consequences. Had the decision gone the way that Lord Justices Atkin and Scrutton wanted, the result would have differently affected not only the employees and ratepayers of Poplar and other local authorities but the structure of municipal government itself. Legislation would have been necessary if the decision was to be changed and that might have been a difficult political exercise. The courts were playing an important part in a situation which was potentially explosive. When it did explode in 1926, the courts were drawn in and the suspicions long held by trade unionists of judicial prejudice against them were reinforced. Astbury J's part seems to have been deliberately interventionist though it is not surprising to find a High Court seeking to reassure employees that they could break the strike without loss to themselves while telling them that they continued it at their peril.

From the mid 1920s the courts began to grapple with the problem of their function in disputes between local authorities and property owners. Inclined as they were, and as they remained, to protect private rights against expropriation or compulsory acquisition and so to insist on meticulous observance of procedural safeguards, they recognized the importance of the public interest in redevelopment and slum clearance schemes. Against the prevailing antagonism of Lord Hewart CJ in *ex parte Davis* (1929)[1] and of many others must be set the sentiment of Viscount Dunedin overruling the Court of Appeal in *ex parte Yaffe*[2] when he said that he was glad to be able to reach that result:

> No one could possibly look at these proceedings without being convinced that they are a genuine scheme for sweeping away an insanitary area and replacing the old by new and sanitary houses. There is no trace of any oblique motive.

But still the courts could not easily stomach the invasion of property rights in the 1930s as the *Errington* decision showed. Their attitudes, their views of the judicial functions in these matters, were largely unformed, politically unsophisticated. They recognized the existence of a public interest but they seemed most unsure of its extent and how it should be accommodated within their traditional range of choices. So they tended to fall back onto the insistence of proper procedures of the kind they were familiar with: the rules of natural justice. And again, this had its political consequences.

The majority decision in *Liversidge* v. *Anderson* (1942) was in keeping with a narrow view of the judicial function and for many its wartime context is a sufficient explanation. But it cast its shadow forward to support Lord Denning's later blanket justification of executive action where national security was involved and to dominate many decisions in the 1970s, 1980s and early 1990s.

We come then to the first pivotal group of decisions strongly influenced by Lord Greene's period as Master of the Rolls from 1937 to 1949. He brought to the central question of the attitude of the senior judiciary to public authorities a more mature political philosophy than any of his twentieth-century predecessors and most of his successors. He put forward a view of the relationship between the three institutions of government which enabled him, as I have tried to explained above, to arrive at a coherent view of the judicial function. And he applied it to the cases that came before him, though I doubt whether he would recognize the applications subsequently made by others of the principles he set down in the *Wednesbury* case. He was concerned to provide a limited basis for judicial review of administrative action. Some of his successors used those principles greatly to extend and enlarge that basis.

The 1950s was a dull period in public law, apart from Kilmuir's excursions to Suez and back. Simonds seems not to have much directed his mind to the problems of law and the state, except to agree that they should be kept separate, although on one occasion he famously and singlehandedly created a new common-law crime, of conspiracy to corrupt public morals.[3] Nor was the Court of Appeal much enlivened by Lord Evershed's tenure as Master of the Rolls (1949–62) although Denning was a member of the court from 1948 to 1957. But the main reason why the 1950s provided few fireworks was that, in this period of relative quiescence in domestic politics, Conservative Governments were governing uncontroversially and the trade unions were still enjoying full employment. It was a decade divided, as Kenneth Morgan entitles it, into two periods, first of Conservative compromise and then of one-nation Toryism. Few major political disputes reached the courts.

The second pivotal period was the 1960s. In 1962, Lord Reid became senior Law Lord in place of Simonds and Lord Denning became Master of the Rolls in place of Evershed. In March 1963, the Lords handed down their decision in *Ridge* v. *Baldwin* and in January 1964 their decision in *Rookes* v. *Barnard*. The new positive, purposive attitudes of the courts began to emerge. It is worth repeating that in every one of the seven major decisions in the 1960s – *Ridge, Rookes, Burmah Oil, Stratford, Padfield, Conway, Anisminic* – the Law Lords reversed the Court of Appeal or its equivalent in Scotland. This was more than a change of style. And in each case the consequences in later years were, in different ways, politically important.

As I have said above, whether this deep change was to be welcomed, in whole or in part, is a political question because it concerns the desirable extent of judicial power. It is indisputable that these cases enlarged that extent and encouraged further enlargement in the 1970s and 1980s.

After the débâcle of *Heaton's* case (1972) when the Law Lords sprang the dockers from prison, and Denning in *Aslef* (1972) found a way round the inconveniences of *Padfield* when trade unions appeared to be able to benefit from that decision, the attitude of the Court of Appeal towards the Labour legislation 1974 to 1979 was so antagonistic that at the end of the decade the Law Lords had to restrain Denning. In 1973 Reid overruled the Court of Appeal in the thalidomide case with the support of Morris, Diplock, Simon and Cross and set the pattern for the extensive press censorship of the 1980s. *Tameside* (1976) built on *Padfield*.

The third pivotal period was that dominated by Lord Diplock and to a lesser extent by Lord Wilberforce from the mid 1970s to the mid 1980s. Judicial attitudes seem to harden remarkably, in a way unprecedented since the courts' attempt to subvert industrial relations legislation in the late nineteenth century. In very quick succession the Law Lords, affirming the Court of Appeal, decided *BSC* v. *Granada* (1980), *Bromley* (1981), *Harman* (1982), *Defence Secretary* v. *Guardian* (1984) and the *GCHQ* case (1984). These decisions were followed by the *Spycatcher* cases, the miscarriages of justice and the public attacks by the senior judiciary on Lord Chancellor MacKay's proposals for reform. By the end of the decade, the reputation of the senior judiciary was lower than at any time this century.

The impact of all these events has meant that the practice of the law and so the judiciary itself has been scrutinized and criticized by the general public to an extent not previously seen in this century. But, more to my present purpose, the attitude of the senior judiciary to the outside world may be in the process of radical change. It is realized that the judicial system has lost much respect and much authority. And no one should be more aware of the dangers of a weakened judicial system than government itself. So it becomes imperative that the senior judges manage as quickly as possible to restore confidence in a reformed system. This will not be easy so serious has been the damage. The role of the judiciary in the political structure is at least to appear to mediate between the organs of the state and the individual so that the legitimacy of the exercise of public power is sustained. When the judiciary is diminished in reputation, that legitimacy is also weakened. It may be that, under a reforming Lord Chancellor, a new Lord Chief Justice and a different Master of the Rolls, the administration of justice – no longer the envy of the world – will, under the stimulus of the recommendations of the report of the Royal Commission in 1993, begin to rebuild its credibility. And it is to be hoped that the attitudes of the senior judiciary to the powers of public authorities will become more principled and more consistent.

Notes

1 See above, p. 21.
2 See above, pp. 21–2.
3 *Shaw* v. *DPP* [1962] AC 220.

Appendix 1
The structure of
the courts

The cases discussed in this book were, in the great majority,
heard in the civil courts. Such cases are begun either in the Queen's
Bench or the Chancery Divisions of the High Court where they
are heard by a High Court judge who is referred to in speech as
'Mr Justice Brown' (or whoever) and in writing as 'Brown J'.
Two or three High Court judges sit together in the Divisional
Court. From the High Court, appeal lies to the Court of Appeal
where three judges sit, often with the Master of the Rolls presiding. Each of the other judges is referred to as 'Lord Justice Brown'
or 'Brown LJ (the plural being Smith and Brown L JJ).' From
the Court of Appeal, appeal lies (if permission is given) to the
Appellate Committee of the House of Lords where five judges sit
together. Each is referred to as 'Lord Brown' and is known as a
Law Lord or Lord of Appeal in Ordinary.

The Lord Chief Justice may preside over the Divisional Court.
The head of the Chancery Division is the Vice-Chancellor. The
Appellate Committee is presided over occasionally by the Lord
Chancellor but in his absence by one of two 'senior' Law Lords
named as Deputy Speakers for judicial purposes. Thus:

House of Lords (Appellate Committee)
(The Lord Chancellor, Lords of Appeal in Ordinary or Law Lords)

↑

Court of Appeal
(Master of the Rolls and Lord Justices of Appeal)

↑

Queen's Bench	Divisional Court	Chancery Division
(High Court judges)	(Lord Chief Justice and High Court judges)	(High Court judges)

Appendix 2
The labour injunction

An injunction is an order of the court which may be issued whenever the court 'finds it just and convenient to do so' requiring the defendant not to commit or not to repeat a wrongful act. So a plaintiff employer or a dissident trade unionist in an industrial dispute may seek an order to prevent or stop a strike or other industrial action claimed to be illegal. But, more importantly in such cases, an interim (or interlocutory) injunction may be sought by the plaintiff to prevent threatened action, pending the determination at the full trial of the question whether the action is legal or not. The basic purpose of the grant of such an injunction is to preserve the status quo until the rights of the parties have been determined at the trial. The grant of such an injunction prevents the defendant trade union or its members from acting at the time they believe will be most effective. Because several months are likely to elapse between the granting of the interim injunction and the full trial, the court's decision whether or not to grant the interim injunction is usually conclusive of the whole matter and the full trial does not take place.

To be granted such an injunction the plaintiff must convince the court that there is 'a serious question' of legality to be tried. The plaintiff's claim must not be frivolous or vexatious and he must also show that he would suffer more harm if the interim injunction were not granted than the defendant would suffer if it were granted. There are further complications[1] but as the law stands the interim injunction is easier for the plaintiff employer to obtain than for the defendant trade union to resist. Most of the injunctions referred to in the text are of this interim kind.

Note

1 See Wedderburn, *The Worker and the Law* (3rd edn, 1986), pp. 684–701.

Bibliography

Adeney, M. and Lloyd, J. 1986. *The Miners' Strike*, London: Routledge & Kegan Paul.

Aubrey, Crispin 1981. *Who's Watching You?* Harmondsworth: Penguin Books.

Bevins, R. 1965. *The Greasy Pole*, London: Hodder & Stoughton.

Blom-Cooper, Louis and Drewry, Gavin 1972. *Final Appeal*, Oxford: Oxford University Press.

Bowley, M. 1945. *Housing and the State 1919–1944*, London: Allen & Unwin.

Branson, N. 1979. *Poplarism 1919–1925*, London: Lawrence & Wishart.

Brown, Phelps H. 1983. *Origins of Trade Union Power*, Oxford: Clarendon Press.

Burnett, John 1986. *A Social History of Housing 1815–1985* (2nd edn) London, Methuen.

Cairncross, Alec 1992. *The British Economy since 1945*, Oxford: Blackwell.

Cairncross, Alec 1985. *Years of Recovery*, London: Methuen.

Callaghan, James 1987. *Time and Chance*, London: Collins.

Clay, H. (ed.) 1955. *The Inter-War Years*, Oxford: Clarendon Press.

Coates, David 1989. *The Crisis of Labour*, Oxford: Philip Allan.

Devlin, Lord 1979. *The Judge*, Oxford: Oxford University Press.

Dickinson, M. 1984. *To Break a Union*, Manchester: Booklist.

Donoughue, Bernard 1987. *Prime Minister*, London: Jonathan Cape.

Donoughue, B. and Jones, G.W. 1971. *Herbert Morrison*, London: Weidenfeld & Nicolson.

Eden, Anthony 1960. *Full Circle*, London: Cassell.

Evans, Harold 1984. *Good Times Bad Times*, London: Weidenfeld & Nicolson.

Ewing, K.D. and Gearty, C.A. 1990. *Freedom under Thatcher*, Oxford: Oxford University Press.

Fine, Bob and Millar, Robert (eds) 1985. *Policing the Miners' Strike*, London: Lawrence & Wishart.

Fysh, M. (ed.) 1989. *The Spycatcher Cases*, London: European Law Centre.

Garside, W.R. 1990. *British Unemployment 1919–1939*, Cambridge: Cambridge University Press.

Hain, Peter 1986. *Political Strikes*, Harmondsworth: Viking.

Harlow, C. and Rawlings, R. 1984. *Law and Administration*, London: Weidenfeld & Nicolson.

Healey, Dennis, 1989. *The Time of My Life*, Harmondsworth: Penguin Books.

Henderson, H.D. 1955. 'Do We Want Public Works?', in H. Clay (ed.) *The Inter-War Years*.

Heuston, R.F.V. 1964. *Lives of the Lord Chancellors 1885–1940*, Oxford: Oxford University Press.

Heuston, R.F.V. 1987. *Lives of the Lord Chancellors 1940–1970*, Oxford: Oxford University Press.

Hewart, Lord 1929. *The New Despotism*, London: Benn.

Holman, Bob 1990. *Good Old George*, Oxford: Lion.

James, Robert, Rhodes 1986. *Anthony Eden*, London: Weidenfeld & Nicolson.

Jowell, J.L. and McAuslan, J.P.W.B. (eds) 1984. *Lord Denning, the Judge and the Law*, London: Sweet and Maxwell.

Kilmuir, Lord 1964. *Political Adventure*, London: Weidenfeld & Nicolson.

Kyle, Keith 1991. *Suez*, London: Weidenfeld & Nicolson.

Lansbury, G. (1928). *My Life*, London: Constable.

Lewis, G. 1983. *Lord Atkin*, London: Butterworth.

Lloyd, Selwyn 1978. *Suez 1956*, London: Jonathan Cape.

Louis, W.R. and Owen, R. (eds) 1989. *Suez 1956*, Oxford: Oxford University Press.

Lucas, Scott W. 1991. *Divided We Stand*, London: Hodder & Stoughton.

Mackintosh, John P. (ed.) 1978. *British Prime Ministers in the Twentieth Century*, vol. ii, London: Weidenfeld & Nicolson.

Maugham, F.H. 1954. *At the End of the Day*, London: Heinemann.

McIlroy, John 1991. *The Permanent Revolution?* Nottingham: Spokesman.

Morgan, K.O. 1990. *The People's Peace*, Oxford: Oxford University Press.

Mullin, Chris 1990. *Error of Judgment*, Swords, Co. Dublin: Poolbeg.

Paterson, Alan 1982. *The Law Lords*, London: Macmillan.

Postgate, R. 1951. *The Life of George Landsbury*, London: Longman.

Prior, Jim 1986. *A Balance of Power*, London: Hamish Hamilton.

Robson, W.A. 1928. *Justice and Administrative Law*, London: Macmillan.

Roth, Andrew 1972. *Heath and the Heathmen*, London: Routledge & Kegan Paul.

Schneer, J. 1990. *George Lansbury*, Manchester: Manchester University Press.

Simpson, A.W.B. 1992. *In the Highest Degree Odious: Detention without Trial in Wartime Britain*, Oxford: Oxford University Press.

Stevens, Robert 1979. *Law and Politics: The House of Lords as a Judicial Body 1800–1976*, London: Weidenfeld & Nicolson.

The *Sunday Times* Insight Team 1979. *Suffer the Children: The Story of Thalidomide*, London: André Deutsch.

The *Sunday Times* Insight Team 1973. *The Thalidomide Children and the Law*, London: André Deutsch.

Taylor, A.J.P. 1965. *English History 1914–1945*, Oxford: Oxford University Press.

Teff, H. and Munro, C. 1976. *Thalidomide the Legal Aftermath*, Farnborough: Saxon House.

Wedderburn, K.W. 1986. *The Worker and the Law* (3rd edn), Harmondsworth: Penguin Books.

Whitehead, Philip 1985. *The Writing on the Wall*, London: Michael Joseph.

Whiteside, Noel 1991. *Bad Times*, London: Faber & Faber.

Wilkinson, Ellen 1939. *The Town That Was Murdered*, London: Gollancz.

Wilson, Harold 1979. *Final Term*, London: Weidenfeld & Nicolson.

Wilson, Harold 1974. *The Labour Government 1964–70*, Harmondsworth: Penguin Books.

Wright, Peter 1987. *Spycatcher*, New York: Viking Penguin.

Young, Hugo 1976. *The Crossman Affair*, London: Hamish Hamilton, Jonathan Cape, and the *Sunday Times*.

Young, Hugo 1989. *One of Us*, London: Macmillan.

General index

Case index